The Playwright & Historical Change

The Playwright &
Historical Change

Dramatic Strategies in BRECHT
HAUPTMANN
KAISER
& WEDEKIND

LEROY R. SHAW

The University of Wisconsin Press 1970
Madison, Milwaukee, & London

Published by
The University of Wisconsin Press
Box 1379, Madison, Wisconsin 53701
The University of Wisconsin Press, Ltd.
27–29 Whitfield Street, London W. 1

Printed in the United States of America by
North Central Publishing Co., St. Paul, Minnesota

ISBN 0–299–05500–0
LC 75–106042

for Rosmarie

Contents

Preface

THE ESSAYS IN THIS BOOK originated in a series of semi-public lectures held in the Spring of 1967 while I was Visiting Professor of German Literature at Trinity College, Dublin. I had been asked to address an audience that would consist of townsmen as well as gownsmen, and the invitation included a generous mandate to discuss "any aspect of modern drama" I might wish. To an American speaking before a group of Irishmen on a literature foreign to them both, the occasion was not without a certain piquancy, particularly since one part of the audience had come to get acquainted with a subject it presumably knew little about, while the other was there to learn something about critical procedures more characteristic of American than of European scholarship. The attempt to meet both these expectations largely accounts for the selection of plays and the point of view from which I chose to regard them; it may also explain the sporadic shifts in tone or approach within individual essays.

The transfer of lecture into essay always brings a temptation to tinker with the original version in the fond hope of improvement. I confess that I could not resist this temptation and have succumbed to it unconscionably. Believing it better to be hung for a sheep than a lamb, I have added evidence, expanded or clarified the text at multiple points, and in general pursued my first thoughts wherever they might lead. The most radical organizational innovation was in expanding the three Dublin discussions into four in order to place the Hauptmann play on a firmer footing. One feature I hope to have preserved in print, if only here and there, is the tone of oral delivery, for the memory of my contact with the Irish audiences is a bright one, and I should like to think I have done my best to honor the rhetorical tradition that makes their public occasions, even at times a series of academic lectures, such a delightful linguistic exercise. The entire effort, in any case, bears witness to an extremely pleasant event and to many happy hours of teaching and learning among the Irish. I am especially grateful to the Professor of German at Trinity, Dr. L. H. C. Thomas, for his kindness in inviting me to give the Dublin lectures; to my former colleague at Trinity, Miss Ita O'Boyle, for reading portions of the manuscript and offering a number of useful suggestions; and in another, no less important way, to the Graduate Council of Dublin University and the Graduate School at the University of Wisconsin–Milwaukee for encouraging me to ready the lectures for publication and providing the wherewithal to make this possible.

LRS

Oak Park, Illinois
January 1970

The Playwright & Historical Change

1

Introduction

THESE STUDIES WERE DESIGNED to provide a fair sampling of German drama in the first quarter of this century — hence one work by each of the period's leading playwrights, ranging from early modern to near contemporary,[1] each of which exhibits a demonstrable correspondence between personal style and predominant literary trend. Not all the plays I selected are masterpieces, to be sure, and they may not even be among the best their authors have to offer; all of them are early works whose peculiar virtue for my purpose lies in their embodying distinctly varied responses to the problem of historical change. The subject, of course, is hardly original; change is inherent in the drama, since it is that aspect of human experience which the genre exists to imitate, and it continues to provide the drama with one of its most durable themes. Yet only in our century, perhaps, which has witnessed more than its share of dramatic happenings, has this fact pene-

1. Excluded is Arthur Schnitzler, whose star has been rising in the last decade but who had to be omitted for lack of space.

trated so deep into general consciousness, forcing our playwrights to deal with change head-on, to probe into its nature or origins, and to try to discover in it new structural possibilities for their medium.

This preoccupation with change has left its mark throughout modern drama. In the plays with which we are concerned here, the problem has been located squarely in its temporal dimension, for the dramatic situation in every case is understood to be the outcome of historical events and presents in concrete form what the playwright regards as significant or fundamental (*Realität*) amid the welter of contemporary circumstance (*Aktualität*).[2] All four of the plays deal with the German condition at a particular juncture in history and with the possibilities open to moral choice, but they differ in their conception of the relationship between actual and real, and consequently in the kind of response they make to it.

Literature (and this is preeminently true of the drama) is intimately related to the business of living — not in the sense that it deals with events directly in order to influence our handling of them, but in the sense that it formulates experience symbolically, testifying to an encounter with reality and to one way of coming to terms with it. As a virtual pattern of experience, a work exists for pure contemplation — this is its nature as an aesthetic construct — but it may also be said to speak both *for* the author, who has transmuted his profound concerns into this particular form, and *to* the reader, whose encounter with the form is the more meaningful the greater its affect upon the quality of his own attitudes and actions.[3] All this

2. These terms, derived from Heinrich Böll, are discussed at more length on p. 13.

3. Perhaps I should add an obvious caution: "Many of the things that a poet's work does for *him* are not things that the same work does for *us* (i.e., there is a difference in act between the poem as being-written and

is tacitly acknowledged with respect to contemporary works, which most of us read with at least one eye open for their bearing on our existence; but when it comes to works of the past, and especially works of the recent past (somehow the less remote a work is in time, the more remote it seems from our needs), we find this less easy to understand and rather difficult to demonstrate. Professional students of literature often seem at a loss in this respect, treating works of the past with the respect we normally reserve for the dead and revering them with that peculiar type of funeral oration we call literary history. Must, and should, this be so? Can we devise no better methods for pointing out the connections between life and art, connections that might make sense even in our academies? The matter has serious implications for all the humanities — to say nothing of our teaching of them — as is quite obvious in those irritating and much abused charges of irrelevance which continue to jar our nerves and ears. The truth, of course, is that literature (and not only great literature) does have its own kind of relevance, which has less to do with the time in which a work is read or written than with its ability to provide answers to the questions raised in any individual work; its relevance consists in formulating and reformulating the human situation in order to supply possible attitudes towards it.

The American philosopher-critic Kenneth Burke has a definition of literature which comes in very handy at this point.[4] Poetry, so the formula goes, is "the adopting of various strategies for the encompassing of situations." The

---

the poem as being-read)." Kenneth Burke, *The Philosophy of Literary Form*, p. 62.

4. Two anthologies of essays by Burke, *Terms for Order* and *Perspectives by Incongruity*, both edited by Stanley Edgar Hyman, make a good introduction to his work. Both titles refer to key Burkean concepts.

phrase occurs in a comprehensive statement on the opening page of *The Philosophy of Literary Form*:

> Critical and imaginative works are answers to questions posed
> by the situation in which they arose. They are not merely
> answers, they are *strategic* answers, *stylized* answers. For
> there is a difference in style or strategy, if one says "yes"
> in tonalities that imply "thank god" or in tonalities that
> imply "alas!" So I should propose an initial working dis-
> tinction between "strategies" and "situations," whereby we
> think of poetry (I here use the term to include any work of
> critical or imaginative cast) as the adopting of various strate-
> gies for the encompassing of situations. These strategies size
> up the situations, name their structure and outstanding in-
> gredients, and name them in a way that contains an attitude
> toward them.

The full range of this definition can hardly be indicated in
a few words, not simply because it is extracted here from
the system to which it belongs — and Burke *has* developed a philosophical system in spite of his freewheeling
dialectic — but also because his general concerns are never
solely (or even primarily) literary. Like all his terms, the
situation-strategy pair was invented to allow him maximum flexibility in analysis. Thus he calls any "document
bequeathed to us by history," the American Constitution
for example, a strategy inasmuch as it offers an "*answer* or
response to assertions current in the situation in which it
arises." [5] Since I cannot be sure my readers are acquainted
with Burke's work, and his terminological twins figure
largely in these essays, it seems necessary to explain the
concept briefly as I understand it.

A situation is any concatenation of circumstances or
state of affairs which appears meaningful to the person experiencing it. What determines its meaningfulness, ac-

5. Burke, *The Philosophy of Literary Form*, p. 93.

cording to Burke, is one's "orientation" or general view of reality: that is, the way in which an individual orders the relationships between things or events and according to which he "rationalizes" his thoughts and actions. Reality, then, is our interpretation, within terms of the orientation, as to what among the totality of things affects us most; it is the name we give "to what things would do to us or for us." And just as, objectively, "different frameworks of interpretation will lead to different conclusions as to what reality is," so, subjectively, it will lead to different accounts of motive, that is, to different explanations as to why we act the way we do. Motives, in this sense, are simply "shorthand terms" for situations.[6] As already noted, the situations of life are reenacted symbolically in the work of literature for the purpose of encompassing them. Hence, in any work, the situation or motive "is equated with the structure of interrelationships within the work itself"; it is "that center about which its structure revolves, or the law of its development." Otherwise expressed, "The motivation out of which [an author] writes is synonymous with the structural way in which he puts events and values together. . . ."[7]

This brings us to strategy, a term whose usual connotations might seem to preclude its use in criticism but which actually make it remarkably appropriate for Burke's purposes. Just as strategy in the military sense is the art of manipulating one's forces in order to confound the enemy and secure results most advantageous to oneself, so in life "one seeks to 'direct the larger movements and operations' in one's campaign of living. One 'maneuvers,' and the maneuvering is an art."[8] The result is one's strategy. In liter-

6. Kenneth Burke, *Permanence and Change. An Anatomy of Purpose,* chap. 2. See especially p. 29.
7. Burke, *The Philosophy of Literary Form,* p. 229.
8. Ibid., p. 257.

ature, then, which is the symbolic reenactment of a life situation, poetic strategies represent the attempt to cope with situations by naming them in a way that allows us to get the best of them. The relation between strategy and stylization is particularly interesting, for as Burke points out, stylization is inevitable the moment we try to express or describe a situation; it involves a choice among possible ways of naming the situation, a choice that reflects our attitude toward it and the course of action implied in the attitude itself. "Stylization pledges to an act." [9] The matter might be illustrated, as Burke is fond of doing, by citing proverbs, which "name typical, recurrent situations." Proverbs which appear to contradict each other, for example, often reflect nothing more than differences in attitude and corresponding differences in strategy. "Consider, for instance, the *apparently* opposite pair: 'Repentance comes too late' and 'Never too late to mend.' The first is admonitory. It says in effect: 'You'd better look out, or you'll get yourself too far into this business.' The second is consolatory, saying in effect: 'Buck up, old man, you can still pull out of this.'" [10]

Burke's terminological pair might be called fraternal rather than identical twins, for although they are the products of a single idea, they are not exactly alike in all respects. They are not synonymous with content and form, respectively; they are rather closer to scene and act, "with each possessing its own genius, but the two fields interwoven." [11] Perhaps the best way to treat their interre-

9. Ibid., p. 129. "To name something [in a certain style] is symbolically to act out a present attitude towards it, in the naming. . . . The value of such naming will not reside so much in the rewards at the time, but in the 'uses' I may subsequently put my nomenclature to." See also Burke's discussion of style and stylization on pp. 109f., 125f.

10. Ibid., p. 256. Burke discusses proverbs under the general rubric of "Literature as Equipment for Living."

11. Ibid., p. 54.

lationship, certainly the most convenient way for critical analysis, is to remember that they refer to symbolic rather than practical actions, to "the *dancing of an attitude*" or a state of mind, rather than to the doing of actual deeds. As Burke puts it in his homely fashion, "a poem about having children by marriage is not the same thing as having children by marriage." [12] He himself prefers to discuss situations and strategies from the standpoint of "the psychology of the poetic act," for "if we try to discover what the poem is doing for the poet, we may discover a set of generalizations as to what poems do for everybody." [13] Hence, in practice, his restriction of situation to the "burden" of a work — that is, to the concern which prompted a poet to write it in the first place — and of strategy to the stylistic-technical means by which that burden has been overcome. "The poet's burdens [are] symbolic of his style, and his style [is] symbolic of his burden."

> I am merely suggesting that, when you begin to consider the situations behind the tactics of expression, you will find tactics that organize a work technically *because* they organize it emotionally. The two aspects, we might say Spinozistically, are but modes of the same substance. Hence, if you look for a man's *burden*, you will find the principle that reveals the structure of his unburdening; or, in attenuated form, if you look for his problem, you will find the lead that explains the structure of his solution. His answer gets its form by relation to the questions he is answering.[14]

The matter might be summarized by saying that the situation of a work interprets reality in a way that itself elicits the strategy by which that situation is encompassed.

I have not set out to apply Burke's ideas in any consistent fashion, nor to explore the range of their meaning criti-

12. Ibid., p. 9.
13. Ibid., p. 62.
14. Ibid., pp. 77f.

cally, nor even to square my findings with his suggestions. The reason is quite simply that none of this was part of my original intention. Certainly there is danger in detaching individual insights from the system to which they belong, yet this seemed to me a risk well worth taking — even adventuresome — since no attempt had previously been made, so far as I know, to apply Burke's methods to the study of German literature. And I regarded the absence of practical criticism on his part as more of a challenge than a deterrent. Those who do not know Burke's work will probably wonder whether I might not have depended too heavily on him; those who do know him well will possibly conclude that I should have known him better. Both have a point, for as I grew more familiar with the aims and methods of Burke's criticism, I found myself attempting, with ever-growing interest, to explore the wider implications of "this newly discovered country in [my] own backyard." [15] In the end, it might well be that this notion of situation and strategy, focussing on the central concept of style, will offer a way out of the impasse that confronts us in the writing of literary history.

A close look at the German-speaking theater reveals it as a peculiar sort of creature which always seems on the verge of dying and yet resolutely refuses to become a corpse. Not so many years ago Fritz Hochwälder, Austria's leading contemporary playwright, compared it to a tubercular patient — glowing with health on the outside but sick and moribund within. By all external signs a flourishing institution, generously subsidized by the state and acclaimed for its brilliant productions, the theater at heart was barren of dramatic substance, its repertory dependent on foreign imports while the native product shied away

15. Stanley Edgar Hyman, "Kenneth Burke and the Criticism of Symbolic Action," *The Armed Vision*, p. 327.

from significant themes and fell short of a level commensurate with international playwriting. Hochwälder's considered diagnosis: severe debilitation from exposure to the *Wirtschaftswunder*, with general lassitude and resultant loss of appetite for solid, homegrown fare.

Critics measuring the theater's pulse today are scarcely more encouraging. A recent report on contemporary German literature states flatly there is no major dramatist writing at the moment and laments the absence of notable plays since Brecht's death in 1956. Even works like Rolf Hochhuth's *Der Stellvertreter* (*The Deputy*) or Peter Weiss's *Die Verfolgung und Ermordung Jean Paul Marats* (*The Persecution and Assassination of Jean-Paul Marat*), which did so much to put German drama in everyone's mouth, are condemned as merely sensational, unfortunate evidence of a "disturbing need for the extreme as suitable matter for theater audiences."[16]

There may indeed be good reasons for downgrading these particular plays, but sensationalism is not one of them. The drama has traditionally veered to extremes, whether it be incest and matricide among the Greeks or genocide and sexual insanity in our own day; and provoking the public conscience is a long honored theatrical prerogative. One might suppose that a rare German success in this respect ought rather to arouse our admiration than give a cause for complaint. Perhaps great plays are few (about as rare, one imagines, as great novels or great poems), but there are still a number of good ones, and not only by Frisch or Dürrenmatt or Hochwälder, but also by younger writers in both East and West — among them Günter Grass, Hans Erich Nossack, and Heinar Kipphardt — who have turned to the drama after making their reputations in other literary genres. Most notably, as

16. Editor's introduction, Brian Keith-Smith, ed., *Essays on Contemporary German Literature*, p. 12.

the Hochhuth and other plays illustrate, the German drama has been hard at work in the last decade trying to perfect a new form, the so-called documentary play, whose artistic deficiencies should not prevent us from acknowledging it as an appropriate — or as some of its adherents think, characteristic — form for our times. That claim may even be right, for the documentary has its counterparts in the American novel and the international film, and its influence on technique extends to many contemporary German works outside the drama as well.

Amid these signs of vitality the appearance of the documentary might be interpreted as preliminary to a coming period of dramatic creativity. Throughout the history of German drama the road to revival has characteristically led through the actualities of contemporary life. Ever since Lessing and the young Schiller, followed by the writers of *Sturm und Drang* and *Das junge Deutschland* and then the naturalists again at the turn of the century, German playwrights have tried again and again to revitalize the life of drama by imitating the drama of life. So the documentarist. Facts in the actual world are studied for clues to the creation of an artistic one, recent historical circumstance determines the subject and informs the techniques of the play. The subject of the documentary is a current or recent historical event, its settings reproduce well-known localities, the dialogue derives largely from protocol or official records, and the characters are modelled on famous (or infamous), sometimes living personalities — all linked together in a kind of deadpan style for the reenactment of a situation that has already taken place. Here, in radical measure, is the latest product of a recurrent trend toward actuality in German drama, a tradition which runs through its history like an underground river, breaking through to the surface whenever imagination seems about to dry up or the changes of history threaten to outrun it.

The function of the documentary today is not altogether unlike that of the drama at the turn of the century. Both are preoccupied with moral uncertainty in the face of reality and both are concerned with the writer's responsibility in such a state of confusion. We shall look at the situation in 1890 in a moment; in the mid-1960s, the central question is the nature of reality itself or where to locate its significant existence. For if the war and its aftermath, as one writer put it, have made most things unreal, then the elemental necessity is to determine what might still be real among what has been left. Apart from physical nature there are two opposite places in which to look. One is within, in a man's immediate personal experience, the private world of his reactions, fancies, or dreams, where the happenings of inner life have the spontaneous quality of truth; the other is in that very different sort of happening, the recorded and irrefutable course of historical events. This latter is the documentarist's choice. To apply a couple of terms made famous by Heinrich Böll, the documentarist looks for reality in actuality, *Aktualität* being what is immediately graspable through events, and *Realität* being what lies hidden behind events, the possibilities they reveal for man's control or moral choice.[17] Now I do not know Böll's opinion of the documentarists, but I suspect it is not altogether positive. For him the two concepts are always kept distinct, so that "reality becomes the result of acts of interpretation of actuality" and the imagination is responsible for careful choice and depiction of event. Of course the documentarist also wants to let his imagination function as accurately as his reportage, but in

17. Heinrich Böll, "Der Zeitgenosse und die Wirklichkeit," lecture, Northwest German Radio, 1953.

practice he limits the scope of actuality to contemporary historical circumstances or political events and seems to assume there is no distinction between these spheres: actuality and reality are coexistent, or even identical.

The documentarist's radical objectivity in method is a logical outcome of his choice. Having obtained a measure of certainty by fixing reality in historical actuality—he now knows where he is and knows the nature of the choices open to him—the documentarist can only maintain his position, or convince others that it is true, through a rigorously consequential presentation. Nothing must distract us from identifying the actualities depicted with the reality they represent. Aesthetically, this seems an extreme version of illusionism, a doctrine that has been advanced time and again in the history of drama. Yet most earlier versions of illusionism had conceived of the stage as the *mirror* of life (playwrights and players act, and the audience reacts, as if what is going on were true), whereas the documentary thinks of the stage as the *record* of life (there is no room for an "as if"; what is seen has happened or is happening, everything is recognizably true, we do not pretend, we acknowledge). Hence the elimination of all those distances normally preserved underneath the surface in illusionist dramaturgy between life and the drama with respect to time, place, or character. In the documentary play, the real and the virtual world are the same: events on stage recapitulate events in history, the time of action coincides with present occurrence, and even the dramatis personae have living counterparts.

All this makes one doubt whether it is still proper to speak of drama in this connection, for having pushed about as far as they can go, the documentarists may well have reversed the very nature of things. Instead of keeping history and drama distinct, the one serving as source and subject for the other, they seem to have amalgamated the concepts, so that life becomes an historical drama and the enactment of it on stage merely a dramatic history. If such is the case, one might want to formulate a whole new series of questions. Is there, for example, an ulterior motive in the documentarist's method? It is difficult to believe otherwise. The situations of the documentary are invariably political, raising issues of great significance for a national or international community; and at the same time moral inasmuch as they probe deeply into individual conduct and attitude. The protodocumentary play, Hochhuth's *Der Stellvertreter*, pricks Christian conscience by analyzing the example set by the Vicar of Christ and his position towards Nazi persecution of the Jews; Kipphardt's *In der Sache J. Robert Oppenheimer* (*In the Matter of J. Robert Oppenheimer*) questions the moral responsibility of scientists who participated in the making of the atomic bomb dropped on Hiroshima. The effect of the documentarist's objectivity is, therefore, a double or even triple one: he achieves clarity for himself as to what is real, he convinces his audience that the picture is true, and he makes it well-nigh impossible for anyone to miss, or dismiss, the moral issues at stake. This combination of dispassionate method and burning purpose — balancing the monstrous course of history against utter impersonality in depicting it, the exposure of inhuman motivation against a ream of irrefutable facts — probably accounts for the documentary's striking effectiveness. And it works nearly as well on the rostrum as in the theatre, as anyone who has ever heard Peter Weiss perform in public knows. As he sits intoning indictments and extracting confessions, his face impassive and the voice impossibly monotonous, Weiss appears like a latter-day Robespierre returning to condemn the Dantons among us for having betrayed the revolution through weakness or lack of staying power, for ignorance or just plain indifference.

Is it revolution the documentarists want? Probably not in the sense of total destruction in order to set up an order of their own. Men who grow up in a time of negatives seldom see an advantage in making further propaganda for nihilism. Yet the documentarists are certainly not content simply to look upon the world in astonished silence and let things be. Change is inevitable and necessary, but it should not be change just for the sake of change and it must lead out of confusion in the direction of positive action. Like other writers of this generation, the German documentarists feel deeply responsible for the future of their country, too sober for mere broadsides or short-term solutions and yet dedicated enough to attack with vigor when they find an identifiable target. For most writers, this is any established pattern that has proved inadequate or false and any which threatens to obstruct the emergence of new structures not yet defined. Thus they are in "revolt against the inhumanity of an industrialized society, the apparent impotence of organized religions, the restricting taboos of their forefathers, the suppression of the individual."[18] It is hard to quarrel with such aims — hard to zero in on them too — and if the shooting has not inspired more champions, perhaps it is because the targets themselves are somewhat outworn; after all, writers have been practicing on them at least since 1890 and hitting bull's-eyes ever since.

Politics do not seem to have interfered with the documentarists' artistic practice, even though most of them have party commitments and are convinced that the artist has a duty — not merely a right but a duty — to use his art for nonaesthetic purposes and to raise his voice outside his work as well, just like any other citizen, by campaigning for a party program, participating in demonstrations,

18. Keith-Smith, *Essays on Contemporary German Literature*, p. 9.

or what not. This interest in public affairs is generally regarded as a good thing, prompting some enthusiasts (not
unnaturally, they are more often journalists than academic
critics) to see in it signs of a new era of literary-political
commitment comparable to that of the 1830s, when a man
of letters like Heine or Georg Büchner risked his life in
trying to be an active maker of history as well as a mere
creator of fictions. The comparison is hardly exact — for
one thing, writers in the West today are not in danger of
anything unless it be what Rilke called "the devious enmity" of success and fame — but it does remind us that the
documentary is very much an historical phenomenon (a
fact about contemporary works which too often eludes
us) and that the documentarists themselves know perfectly well the tradition they belong to. The mention of
Georg Büchner also establishes another link with the beginning of this century, for Büchner, who died as early as
1837, was only discovered in the 1880s and became then,
as he is in even greater degree now, an idol of the age.
The documentarists' interest in him is easy to understand.
His *Dantons Tod* (*Danton's Death*), for example, set a
pattern for analyzing revolutionary change and for investigating the moral choices in a critical historical situation.
Yet it is doubtful that either of Büchner's protagonists
would be an acceptable hero to the documentarists. Robespierre, the moral ascetic, would be admired for his
dedication but rejected for his inhumane, cold-blooded fa-
naticism; and the epicurean Danton would be rejected for
forsaking the revolution although admired as a full-bodied
human being. Not they, but Büchner himself is the documentarists' hero: Büchner the playwright for reconciling
the claims of life with the claims of art and inventing the
formal means to demonstrate the interaction between
them; and Büchner the spirited, protesting youth who was

able to fuse the separate skills of artist, scientist, and political engagé in a single faculty for pragmatic action.

Mention of Büchner brings me back to my theme. Not only the documentarists claim him, so do many other writers of this generation. Not only was he an idol in 1890, but in every generation since. Even among those writers who deliberately oppose the tradition of actuality, he has served as a source of renewed inspiration. There are many reasons why this should be so, but surely it is in part because Büchner has continued to supply answers for a perennial problem in drama, the problem of how to determine the nature of historical change and of how to cope with the realities it brings in its wake. This is also the problem of these essays. I want to concentrate upon the period roughly marked by the dates 1890 to 1925 and discuss four well-known German plays, each of which treats the problem of change in a different way, the problem itself arising from changes in historical circumstances. The plays by Hauptmann and Wedekind are complementary in that they offer alternative responses to what I shall call the era of transition; the plays by Kaiser and Brecht offer another set of contrasting responses to what I shall call the era of anarchy. Discussion of these works is not intended to substitute for a history of German drama in this period, but the sequence, studied from this point of view, does reveal certain unmistakable lines of development. The Hauptmann play records the anguish of a generation stymied by uncertainties in the face of collapsing values; the Brecht makes an effort to redefine the very nature of events and affirms the positive value of organized doubt. Within this relatively short span of time lack of faith was replaced by confidence in method, concern with substance gave way to determination of structure, and an enervating preoccupation with the past was discarded in favor of a defiant thrust toward the future. In the first two essays

something will be said of the various ways in which the
dramatists regarded and treated the relationship between
the actual and the real; all the essays focus on how a general historical condition has been transmuted into a dramatic situation that embodies the playwright's special
concerns, and attempt to delineate the strategic means he
has devised for encompassing it.

2

The Strategy of Compassion
Gerhart Hauptmann's
Einsame Menschen

LIKE TODAY, the historical situation around 1890 was
marked among other things by a crisis concerning the
nature of reality and the real. Throughout much of the
nineteenth century, the so-called age of materialism, the
real had been recognizable in the solid and substantial objects all around one. A fact was a fact, appearances did
not deceive, the truth was visible, and all that mattered
lay in matter, in what one could see and taste and measure. These things were certain and about them there was
no need for doubt. Confidence in the social order was no
less secure, for its manners and morals seemed inviolable
and its institutions had long since settled on a rationale. In
Germany after 1870, there was the additional security provided by a new-forged political unity, by burgeoning cities and an expanding empire, and by the knowledge that
though government might be paternal, or even autocratic,
it would remain in office to guarantee the safety, security
and complacency of its citizens. Nor did men need to fret
unduly about the caprices of a God whom Ludwig Feuer-
bach and David Friedrich Strauss had cut down to human

dimensions; reason was able to put things in their proper place and the instruments of science could be relied on to smooth out discomfort and distress eventually. To be sure, disturbances had taken place and dissatisfactions had been aired, but there were only faint echoes of these in literature, and in the theatre, from mid-century onward only a house of diversion, the spirit of the age was embodied in the Duke of Meiningen's famous troupe as it travelled about the country performing Shakespeare and the German classics, good "safe" plays offering a monumental image of the present in the trappings of the past. In the Meiningen productions things alone were real: actors staggered under real armor, wore costumes of genuine brocade and accurate historical styling, sat at tables of solid oak and made their exits through slammable doors, met their enemies on stage with smoking cannon, and fought their battles with every realistic device short of real blood.

By century's end, it was obvious that this secure "real" world was already changing. The expansion of trade, industry, and empire had brought forth new types of citizens whose very presence upset the normal social order: the *Bürger* had lost his place as first in the realm, usurped by the monied bourgeois, while the cities had spawned masses and creatures of misery which not even socialistic legislation was able to banish. Bismarck's resignation in 1890 left a wobbly ship of state and shook the trust in political stability, and as the news spread out from Basel that a mad philosopher had dared proclaim the death of God, the fear that this Absolute had really disappeared caused every inferior brand of authority to scramble for position. The great chain of hierarchies began to rattle. Even the sciences, which had risen to glory proving the claims of matter, seemed to desert firm ground as they delved into such unsightly phenomena as the subcon-

scious mind, invisible wave lengths and radiation. Voices
of the irrational rose to question the reign of reason. Suddenly there were no certain certainties any longer, only
doubts and fears in the face of change. Europe had en-
tered on an age of transition.

It was a decisive moment in history and German literature rose from its torpor and strove to match the occasion.
According to the official records, the drama was reborn at
three o'clock on a Sunday afternoon, October 20, 1889, the
date and the hour when Gerhart Hauptmann's *Vor Sonnenaufgang* (*Before Dawn*) was presented by the Freie
Bühne on a rented stage in Berlin. Enough smoke was
sent up on that occasion to becloud literary histories ever
since. Performance and play were both shockers. Casting
his work in the mode then fashionable in France, Russia,
and Scandinavia, Hauptmann focused with relentless and
crass detail on the corrupting effects of industrial exploitation in a small Silesian village — alcoholism, conspicuous
waste, sexual offenses, and as one of the characters himself
puts it, "degeneration down the whole line." The subscrip-
tion audience responded to this first German naturalistic
play with appropriate gusto. Alternately jeering and
cheering the scandalous goings-on, they finally broke up
the performance in the last act when a doctor rose from the
auditorium, forceps in hand, to offer his assistance in the
birth of a baby offstage. Probably no one, least of all Hauptmann himself, could have predicted the impact of this
occasion; even old Theodor Fontane, meditating on the
pallid and milk fed appearance of the young author, was
led to wonder aloud at the discrepancy between murder-
ers and their deeds.[1] It hardly mattered that this first
product of modern German drama was an ugly and under-

1. Theodor Fontane, *Causerien über Theater*, ed. Paul Schlenther,
pp. 309–10.

developed child; its mere existence signified the end of
sterility and a legitimate German claim to the inheritance
of European dramaturgy. And the proud father was en-
couraged by the momentous event to follow through with
two more offspring of the same kind. In 1890 he published *Das Friedenfest* (*The Reconciliation*), in 1891 *Einsame Menschen* (*Lonely Lives*). When the latter was accepted by the Deutsches Theater, a state-run institution,
the genre had clearly "arrived" in Germany and Hauptmann was acknowledged as its foremost playwright.

Of these three earliest plays, *Einsame Menschen* gives
the clearest dramatic statement of the problems arising
from the historical situation around 1890 and offers a strategic response quite characteristic of the early Hauptmann. We shall also find that the "dilemma" he sets up for
his protagonist is a symbolic projection of the moral burden he shared with many other writers of that generation.
The play presents two branches of the same family: the
younger represented by Käthe and Johannes Vockerat, a
scientist living in the shadow of Berlin on the Müggelsee;
the older by his fundamentalist parents who are at home
in rural Silesia. The younger Vockerats have just had a
son, and Johannes, although he no longer believes in the
ritual, has reluctantly consented to the infant's baptism. A
tense emotional state has developed and this soon becomes keener when Anna Mahr, a student of sociology
from Zurich, appears and is invited to stay a few days as
the Vockerats' guest. Anna sympathizes with Johannes'
predicament and supplies him with the moral support he
misses in his own wife, Käthe. As the friendship between
them deepens, the rapport between husband and wife di-
minishes to a point where the marriage itself seems threatened. The parents feel compelled to intervene with the
warning that Johannes is close to committing adultery in
his heart and has already caused irreparable damage to

his wife and family. Soon Anna is obliged to depart, and Johannes — having failed to convince her or his family that their friendship does not infringe on marriage but actually anticipates an ideal future type of relationship between men and women — leaves a note indicating that he intends to drown himself in the Müggelsee.

Everything in *Einsame Menschen* testifies to the experience of an individual caught in a transitional situation, suffering the debilitating moral consequences of his inability to accept the inevitable separation between old and new. Although members of the same family, the Vockerats are no longer sure they truly belong to each other, and although all share the same household, none are completely at home in it. The attempt of the younger Vockerats to find their own way of life is impeded by their allegiance to values inherited from the past, while the attempt of the parents to realize their hopes in the children is impeded by failure to recognize those values in another guise. The intermingling of inherent contradiction is symbolized by physical details: the setting is a villa halfway out in the countryside but near the metropolis, and the Vockerats' living room displays photographs of Käthe's father, a pastor in his vestments, as well as portraits of Darwin and Ernst Häckel. Still able to converse and live alongside each other, the generations touch explosive material whenever they exchange views on any important topic — on the one side, the ideals of science, social egalitarianism, and the notion that art must be realistic and socially oriented; on the other, the language of religion, paternalism, and the notion of art as innocuous entertainment.

To these actualities of the milieu Hauptmann adds the actualities of individual behavior, showing the nature of the crisis most intensely in Johannes, who as a creative man has come closest to the point of decision and no return. Johannes is a deeply fragmented person. Torn between the convictions of his mind and the dictates of his heart, he wants to act according to the knowledge gleaned from his scientific studies but is unable to break away emotionally from the beliefs in which he was brought up and which his wife and parents still cherish. The indecision reflects his uncertainty about ultimate authority; he cannot accept the traditional sources, yet is afraid of the consequences in pledging unreserved allegiance to the new. Hence his unpredictable, seemingly unmotivated and thoroughly erratic behavior, at one moment full of tender consideration, at the next almost brutishly stand-offish. His relationships with everyone become disturbed, and as the pressure of decision-making mounts, he begins to question the very nature of friendship, marriage, and filial devotion. Neither Johannes nor his family can quite explain the situation, and indeed it *is* irrational since it involves the breakthrough of emotions and feelings not previously suspected and the assertion of desires which the conventional scheme of values was not designed to accommodate. The net effect is to make Johannes a moral cripple, unable to act on his principles, unable to act at all except with the defiant gesture of would-be suicide, a victim of pieties or, as Anna Mahr describes him, a victim of his own conscience. Nowadays we would probably label him quite bluntly a neurotic — unwilling to change himself or adjust to outer necessity, incapable of saying yes or no, more obsessed with his condition than bent on exploring ways of getting around it. A more charitable, perhaps more accurate term to describe his condition, and that of the other "lonely lives" in the play, would be demoralization, in the full sense of that word: his morale is low because he is disoriented about values and mores, and because of the disorientation he has drifted into a moral limbo, unable to act or decide on his own.

Like the documentary, *Einsame Menschen* faces the

problems of a transitional era and searches for reality in the actualities of contemporary life. Yet Hauptmann interprets "reality" and "actuality," or the relationship between them, quite otherwise than the documentarist, and differs also in his notion of the drama's function when confronted with the facts of historical change. The documentarist looks upon transition as a period between nihilism and the positive future, an undetermined condition but alive with dynamic change and movement. Uncertainty results because decisions must be made among a fullness of possibilities. Contemporary man, as the documentarist sees him, is like a motorist who has been driving at great speed through a grotesque landscape and suddenly finds himself at a huge and complex traffic junction. The lane narrows and he must quickly choose, amid the mass of onrushing vehicles, which of the several routes before him will take him somewhere he might want to go. The generation of 1890, on the other hand, thought of transition paradoxically as a static state of suspension, hovering between old and new orders, the one not yet out of sight, the other not yet in view. It was as if man in that time had drifted unawares into a maze so bewildering to his senses that he could no longer find a way in or a way out. The changes he saw were nothing more than altered arrangements of the same pattern, confirming his perplexity without providing a solution. His uncertainty lay in the absence of orientation.

Faced with *his* historical situation the documentarist uses the play to discover leads to reality in actual events. He seeks clarity about what has happened for the sake of discovering what must be — the facts of today are the basis for determining the acts of tomorrow. History and politics are essential to the documentarist because actual events are true events and, therefore, sure indicators of the real. The changes of history contain a promise of inevitable change to come; the knowledge of the immediate past provides firm factual ground from which to assess the situation. As Hans Magnus Enzensberger, not a documentarist himself, says of contemporary poetry,[2] so we may say of the documentary play that its task is to point out "states of affairs" (*Sachverhalte*) so that the very process of understanding — it is not quite clear how — will bring about alteration. Faced with *his* historical situation, on the other hand, the playwright of 1890 used the drama primarily to express his shock and hurt at finding himself in such a predicament and to explore some of its implications. Hence his need, not to record events but to define them, not to deal with what had happened but to discover what was actually taking place. Changes in the historical situation had caught the generation of 1890, the dramatist as well as his public, napping and unawares; it was imperative to realize the cause and import of current events and to gauge their effects on individual men and women. Thus psychological circumstances and states of mind, rather than deeds and decisions, were the best clues to reality, and the drama had to sharpen its analytical tools in order to expose their meaning. The method was essentially diagnostic.

Perhaps this is one reason for Hauptmann's working on such a small dramatic scale. Unlike the documentarist, who favors a broad canvas, picturing the portentous actions of important men as they move within the councils of the high and mighty, the early Hauptmann concentrated on the narrow circle of family and everyday event, an intimate world in which significance is measured within the range of personal misfortune, a familiar world delineated by the things of everyday life, populated with

2. Cited by Patrick Bridgwater, "Hans Magnus Enzensberger," *Essays on Contemporary German Literature*, pp. 242f.

the types of people known from one's work and society, speaking the language of street and kitchen, thinking in the quotidian terms of current social patterns and problems. The crisis of transition was to be made real and recognizable as part of one's immediate experience. This, rather than any deep conviction that the consequences of transition weighed more heavily on the family than on other institutions, was probably the main reason for Hauptmann's setting his play among the professional bourgeois class. This was his own milieu, he understood the Johannes Vockerats around him, and he knew also that his audience would understand and identify with the type. The drama of *Einsame Menschen* was dedicated to "those who have already lived it."

What strategy does Hauptmann propose for encompassing this situation? A first glimpse detects no strategy at all, for *Einsame Menschen* seems to lack answers to the problems it raises and its surface suggests deliberate avoidance of any artistic manipulation or design. The careful delineation of speech and actions, the detailed description of tangible "real" things in the scene, leave an impression of life observed in the raw, dispassionately and accurately, without interference from the playwright or distortion of the truth through special dramatic procedures and a point of view. A genuine "slice of life," therefore, according to the tenets of the prevailing naturalistic mode. Hauptmann's skill in creating such illusions has been much admired. Whether or not he always carried a notebook about with him, as contemporary caricatures claimed, he certainly had a unique ability to register the externals of existence and to render these convincingly in dialogue and scene. And his natural bent here was given a scientific cast in the eighties and nineties by his study of socio-psychological documents, among others the works of the Swiss psychiatrist Auguste Forel. Hauptmann himself would

never have called *Einsame Menschen* the case history of a
neurotic; nevertheless his portrait of Johannes Vockerat
bears many earmarks of that form — in its selection of detail indicating an overall pattern or syndrome, for example, and in its suggestion of causes deducible from symp-
tomatic effects. A play so written might appear to lack
answers, but there must be no doubt about its truthful depiction of a recognizable state of affairs.

Of course, the ostensible elimination of a point of view,
at least in any halfway respectable play, itself reveals a
type of strategy, and a playwright who pretends to pull no
tricks, like a magician, must be an exceedingly clever manipulator in order to conceal his sleight of hand. Hauptmann had the necessary talent to bring this off, but his
knowledge of the métier was not yet faultless and he had
apparently not yet realized that magic, like any of the
other arts, has only questionable validity beyond the situation it is originally designed for. Our suspicion that
Hauptmann might have had something up his sleeve
arises initially from his choice of subject matter. Not just
any situation would do, it must be one with a built-in
emotional charge; not merely a familiar situation, but one
that was sure to move the heart, if not the head. But how
can sentiment be reconciled with objectivity or pathos
with an analytical history? I do not think these were only
concessions to taste, or that Hauptmann, instinctive dramatist that he was, sensed rightly that mere description was
not enough to make a drama; though objective narrative
might be proper to the strategies of science, it would not
be sufficient for the crasser needs of drama. On the contrary, the sentimentality and pathos of *Einsame Menschen*
are just as integral as the play's surface objectivity and
just as essential to its strategy. And if these tones are un-
marked signs of artistic manipulation, what are we to say
of the structural form barely concealed beneath the gloss

of contemporaneity, a form so familiar to playgoers at the time that it could easily pass unnoticed? *Einsame Menschen* not only adopts Ibsen's sophisticated analytical form, the *Drama des reifen Zustandes*, according to which the appearance of an outsider triggers exposure of the situation and prompts analysis of how it all came about; it also employs this structure consciously for artful purpose. That purpose is to establish a dilemma. To Johannes Vockerat transition means an unresolvable predicament: there is no way out; circumstances have overpowered his will to carry on. Even the outsider of this play, the prescient Anna Mahr, whose presence seems to promise salvation (and might have saved a hardier male), is not allowed to alter the situation and is herself eventually filled with doubt about her ability, or right, to function as Johannes's rescuer. Clearly, the end was designed and the structure made to support it.

Now I do not wish to accuse Hauptmann of dramatic hypocrisy, as if one of his hands were building a play for emotional effect while the other pretended to make an objective study; possibly the left hand did know what the right one was doing and the ambidextrous playwright was actually controlling them both all along. What *is* of interest in this combination — and might repay comparison with the documentary's way of fusing purpose and dispassion — is what it tells us about the strategy of Hauptmann's play. It was said that *Einsame Menschen* seems to offer no solution for Johannes's problem. Yet in the fourth act, as a parting word of comfort, Anna Mahr does suggest one way of averting possibly serious consequences from his predicament. Referring to their frustrated hopes of breaking the deadlock between old and new through a new type of human relationship, Anna asks Johannes to think of the situation *sub specie evolutionis*. "Nehmen wir mal an," she says,

"—ganz im Allgemeinen—ein neuer, vollkommenerer Zustand wird von jemand vorempfunden. Dann ist er vorläufig im Gefühl — eine überzarte, junge Pflanze, die man schonen und wieder schonen muß. [. . .] Daß das Pflänzchen sich auswächst, während wir leben, das dürfen wir nicht hoffen. Wir können sie niemals groß werden sehn, ihre Früchte sind für andere bestimmt. Auf die Nachwelt den Keim bringen — das können wir vielleicht."[3]

The implications of Anna's organic image are clear. She suggests that Johannes transplant his knowledge of natural evolution to the human condition, recognizing that change, which is inherent in the physical world, also governs the social sphere, despite appearances to the contrary. The present moment might seem static, nevertheless it had resulted from change, and change would ensure that the future in its turn would be different from the past. Anna admits that men cannot determine developments, but she feels that men can influence these by their patient nurturing of hope and dream, the seeds of what might yet take shape. In the long run the course of evolution would be to man's advantage — not at the present moment, of course, but definitely sometime; and if not for any specific individual, then certainly for mankind.

Anna's words are meant to comfort Johannes and bolster his stamina with a scientific doctrine to which they both subscribe. One would expect him to grasp at this straw, yet the instant Anna is gone Johannes scribbles his suicide note and rows out onto the lake. (Whether he actually drowns himself, or is merely trying to frighten his

3. "Let us assume, just in general now, that someone anticipates a new and more nearly perfect condition. For the time being it's just a feeling, a young and very tender plant, which must be protected, time and time again. [. . .] We can hardly hope that the little plant will attain full growth in our lifetime. We can never see it mature; its fruits are destined for others. But we can, perhaps, preserve the seed for posterity."

family, is left up in the air.) Obviously, he cannot, or will not, make use of the idea for coping with his own situation. At this point one begins to wonder. Anna — and I suspect, most of us — would probably consider Johannes's suicide, threatened or actual, as quite unnecessary. It is not inevitable as the result of actions previously taken, and it is not dictated by a true dilemma, for if the situation is really transitional then it will pass away, and if serious consequences can be avoided through a different way of regarding the situation, then the situation itself is not insoluble. It is also obvious, however, that accepting Anna's point of view would completely wreck the play, for it would mean Johannes's salvation and prevent the play from proceeding to its "tragic" conclusion. If only in a dramaturgical sense, then, Hauptmann had to keep Johannes from grasping at Anna's proferred straw. Why then did he complicate matters by manufacturing that possibility in the first place?

Several assumptions are possible. We might assume that Hauptmann himself did not intend his audience to take Anna's arguments seriously. Yet if this were true, he would have been playing with fire, for although an author's viewpoint is not usually the same as a character's opinion (and certainly neither should be confused with the strategy embodied in any particular work), it is also true that any indication of disbelief in evolution would have put Hauptmann on the wrong side of the fence at a time when its truth was generally taken for granted and would have seriously prejudiced our impression of Johannes and Anna as enlightened human beings. A more likely assumption is that Hauptmann *was* serious about the idea, but wanted to show that Johannes, under the mounting pressure of circumstances and at the highly charged moment when his last hope was departing, is simply not capable of perceiving its effectiveness or pertinence in his case. This assumption would account for the scientist's rejection of an idea he believes in, and yet preserve the seemingly dilemmic nature of his situation by placing its roots (if not its origins) in character rather than circumstances. As to which might be cause and which effect, Hauptmann is characteristically vague; it was enough to show the interaction of these actualities, to demonstrate that Johannes *is* the child of his age and that the most negative aspects of this period of flux appear in him as moral uncertainty and the inability to carry on. The only trouble with this assumption, valid as far as it goes, is that it still leaves the problem of the play's strategy undefined and does not explain why Hauptmann should have let Anna propose her rejected solution in the first place.

Let us recall the circumstances once more. *Einsame Menschen*, we said, was addressed to a generation in transition, a time in which accelerating historical events made the presence of change undeniably clear without establishing precisely what was taking place or which changes were accomplished facts. The nature of developments was not yet fully determined nor had the extent of their effects been accurately measured. The deadwood of cultural lag lay everywhere. Established forms of existence were reluctant, as always, to accommodate the new and alien forces, and reluctance degenerated into opposition whenever men rose to protect their vested interests. The paradoxical result was a changing way of life not felt as an evolution from one condition into another but as a static state of suspension between old and new, between something that would not die and something that had not yet been born. For the young bourgeois of 1890, and of course for the writers who also belonged to this class, this was an intolerable situation. They had been caught up in the times and were excited by the promise of progress, yet everything in their background cautioned against committing themselves to an uncertain course. It was difficult enough for most of them to accept that the "real" entailed change; it was excruciating not to know what of the old would still remain and what of the new eventually prevail; and, to many of them, it seemed downright impossible to support changes that might bring the destruction of values they had grown up with and still acknowledged as part of their way of life. The counterpart of cultural lag was psychological disorientation, the problem of how to adjust to the actualities of change without destroying the fabric of one's normal existence. The result was demoralization in the widest sense of that term.

The effects of this situation have been carefully gauged in *Einsame Menschen*: confusion as to the sources of authority, intrusion of the irrational, fragmentation of personality, uncertainty in one's relationships with family and friends. For Hauptmann's protagonist, the situation looks like a genuine dilemma; he believes himself caught by circumstances without an acceptable way out. To the other characters in the play, however, and most notably to Anna Mahr, who is still able to observe him from the point of view of an outsider, Johannes's predicament is less a dilemma than a psychological quandary. In Anna's eyes, he is really a victim of his own conscience, afraid to ally himself with change because it would mean violating his inherited system of pieties, unable to break loose and make his own way lest he be cut off from his roots. In any case Johannes stands alone in a moral limbo, incapable of making a crucial decision while the symptoms of transition fester on in him like gangrene, eating away at his will to live. When he goes off to his suicide — if indeed he does commit suicide — it is not so much out of choice as out of failure to conceive of an alternate course.

In creating this situation Hauptmann undoubtedly aimed at arousing sympathy, and in fact *Einsame*

Menschen did much to establish his once-popular reputation as *der Dichter des Mitleids*, the poet of compassion and suffering — a phrase taken ambiguously to refer both to his own tenderness of heart and to the response he hoped to elicit from his audiences. Perhaps we have a clue here to the play's elusive strategy. *Mitleid*, of course, contains the double sense of "compassion for" and "suffering with." It is the quality which allows one to feel what someone else feels, to share with another the emotions that a person experiences in himself, and which requires an empathic ability to sense another human being's predicament and identify with him by vicariously participating in his suffering. Now, as we saw, Hauptmann took no little pains in *Einsame Menschen* to facilitate such identification, both by dedicating his drama "to those who have already lived it" and by creating a fictional world immediately recognizable to the bourgeois professional class to which he and the larger part of his audience belonged. *Mitleid* was still the great residual virtue of that class, and Hauptmann's attempt to revive this "universal and natural quality of human nature,"[4] was based on the conviction he derived from Schopenhauer (the principal source of his early *Weltanschauung*) that *Mitleid* was the core of human morality and offered the best hope for restoring a firm ethical foundation to a culture already threatening to collapse in uncertainty and moral doubt. At a time when men and women no longer knew what should command their allegiance and were confused by the discrepancy between values and the forms designed to embody them, *Mitleid* promised to be a binding force for society, keeping it stable in spite of upsets and disturbances, joining men and women in reciprocity, comforting them with the

---

4. Arthur Schopenhauer, "Über die Grundlage der Moral," *Sämtliche Werke*, 3:602.

knowledge that although they might not know where they were going on the becalmed sea of transition, at least they were all together in the same boat.

Strategically, the ethic of *Mitleid* became a way of responding to a situation which in itself seemed to preclude any satisfactory answers. It substitutes the motions of the heart for the motions of the external world and time, transferring the seat of motivation from without to within, turning the oppressive force of passive suffering into the emotional force of compassion or suffering with. The man who is moved to *Mitleid*, like the man who is moved by it, gains the advantage of enlisting himself on the side of virtue without the necessity of committing himself to a specific course of action; in having *Mitleid* he demonstrates the presence of sentiment without running the risk of failure in acting upon it. *Mitleid* ennobles even the passive man. The peculiar appeal of this strategy to Hauptmann, as we shall see, lay in the fact that the public function of his play coincided with his private needs. Although it is generally true that "many of the things a poet's work does for *him* are not things that the same work does for *us*," [5] in the case of *Einsame Menschen* Hauptmann neatly disposed of the personal burden history had laid upon him by directing his "answer" to an audience that had already experienced the situation in their own lives.

The public aspect of Hauptmann's strategy is a response to the desperate longing at the time for *Anderswerden* — a change of condition — within an apparently unmoving and unmovable state. [6] Itself incapable of bringing about reform or making things otherwise, *Mitleid* nevertheless creates the mental or spiritual climate

5. Kenneth Burke, *The Philosophy of Literary Form*, p. 62.
6. The longing for *Anderswerden* is heard in all Hauptmann's early works, most explicitly in *Das Friedensfest (The Reconciliation)*, where the word or its variants occur repeatedly.

for improvement; it might be compared to the loving care which Anna suggests to Johannes as indispensable for the full growth of a "young and very tender plant." Hauptmann himself had only the foggiest notion of how *Mitleid* might produce practical results; he is reported to have said of *Die Weber* (*The Weavers*), for example, the play immediately following this one, that he hoped merely to affect people's feelings by the play, to arouse sympathy among those who were better off so that reforms might eventually be brought about.[7] However vague his program, it is clear that *Einsame Menschen* aims at effects outside the play. Like most of Hauptmann's early works, it is exemplary in the sense that it illustrates and is addressed to circumstances beyond those transmuted into the dramatic structure of the work itself. Perhaps the process he had in mind might be explained this way: the drama is to function as a kind of mirror which reflects the historical situation and at the same time gives back to the people who look into it a true image of themselves. The fictional world is drawn from the actual state of affairs and returned to it again so that the audience will recognize its own experience and be moved to do something about it. The strategy defers action, referring and transferring it to another time and place; all activity is focussed on potentiality. Changing the metaphor rather abruptly, the effect is like that of a time bomb that is set to explode later and leave its mark on someone else; the advantage to the maker is that his role preserves him from any immediate aftereffects.

Perhaps this accounts sufficiently for the peculiar combination of objectivity and pathos which troubled us ear-

7. Hauptmann apparently said this in the course of an interview with reporter Charles Henry Meltzer of the *New York World* during his first visit to the United States in 1894. A German version of his statements is given in *Gerhart Hauptmann: Die Weber*, ed. Hans Schwab-Felisch, p. 98.

lier. The objectivity shows a conscientious wish to diagnose the situation accurately and to suggest that rational
procedures were needed to cope with it; the pathos arises
from the playwright's emotions about the situation and his
desire to charge his witness-participants with a like sense
of urgency. Typically, there is little attempt in *Einsame
Menschen* to keep these factors distinct: they seem to
merge in a way of thinking or feeling according to which
all things can be explained rationally and rational explanation will itself strike at the heart. Having been moved
by compassion himself, Hauptmann through the passion-
ate honesty of his case history would be able to move others to a like response.

A strategy based on *Mitleid* is irreproachably humane,
of course, and takes its place in the history of modern German drama as a first, if somewhat primitive, attempt to
bridge the gap between thought and feeling — sometimes
called "the dissociation of sensibility" [8] — which began to
reveal itself in European literature during the last quarter
of the nineteenth century. Yet the strategy might be criti-
cized on both aesthetic and moral grounds. We have said
that Hauptmann directed his play at an audience with the
intention of influencing its own situation as represented in
the play and that he justifies his drama by tailoring it to
immediate actual needs. As a consequence, his answers
seem to be made for people outside the play rather than
for the characters within it, and the moral decisions in-
cumbent upon the dramatis personae, which they do not
make because the playwright insists on establishing their
condition as a dilemma, are transferred to the spectators
in dress circle or gallery. From a technical point of view,
the fault lies in the attempt to carry out a nondramatic

8. Wm. Van O'Connor, Introduction to *Sense and Sensibility in Modern
Poetry*.

purpose within the limits of conventional dramaturgy. It is not necessary to agree wholeheartedly with Peter Szondi, who argues brilliantly (if rather arbitrarily) that the drama as a genre is a self-contained autonomous world independent of anything outside itself,[9] in order to perceive that a strategy must, above all, be pertinent to the situation given in the play. Historical circumstances may certainly provide matter for the drama; they may even guide the manipulation of stylistic or structural elements *as long as* that manipulation is carried out according to the determining law of development in the play and functions to reveal the strategy devised for encompassing that situation. But more or less than this is apt to undermine the impact of the work. Thus, when actuality is used to get at reality it must not break the fictional world by calling attention to itself for its own sake or by forcing an audience to take account of real life circumstances while it is still preoccupied with the situation of the play. We know that drama relates to life, and may also influence our attitude towards it, but it does this best, not by foisting a policy on the viewer, but by fashioning a pattern complete and significant in itself which the audience can grasp and then take issue with. A play which separates strategic decisions from the specific dramatic situations that call for such decisions surrenders its claim to autonomy and subordinates its meaning to temporary, extradramatic truth. In the case of *Einsame Menschen*, the danger of this outwardly directed procedure has been confirmed by the play's short-lived history on the stage; what was once so *zeitgemäß* now seems merely *zeitgebunden*, not only dated but irrelevant, a work too indirect in its aims to be effective and too parochial to outlive the circumstances it describes or the people for whom it was written.

9. Peter Szondi, *Theorie des modernen Dramas*, pp. 14f.

The moral fault of Hauptmann's play may be effectively restated in terms of a metaphor drawn from medicine. The strategy appears then to function something like this: an expiring patient is put on view in the operating theatre while a master physician demonstrates the nature of the disease for the benefit of a watching audience which is presumed to be afflicted with the same malady and must be informed about the measures it might take in order to relieve its own suffering. Melodramatic as it may sound, the metaphor is not farfetched, for health and normality, the "natural" state of man in all its aspects, was a primary concern of the transitional generation and most especially of the playwrights who were trying to gauge the contemporary social and moral predicament. (It is no accident, as we shall see, that the term *naturalism* eventually prevailed in literary history as the most suitable description for expressing this concern.) For Hauptmann, the metaphor seems to have had a special attraction. Even in his first play, there is a gynecologist, Dr. Schimmelpfennig, who comes close to expressing the point of view I have been discussing here. The reason, I think, is that medicine claims to be both a science and an art — the accurate diagnosis of a man's condition and the skillful application of available knowledge to his healing. Furthermore, no one puts facts to better use than the doctor and no one can make a more solid claim to serving mankind. Best of all, a doctor's status is not disturbed by his occasional failure to coordinate science with art, nor even, at times, to save the patient from death. After all, in medicine there is no line of absolute certainty from diagnosis to cure. A doctor's prescription follows the laws of cause and effect but cannot be sure of their immutable operation or results; and unless he speaks for psychological effect (or is very rash indeed) the doctor will never guarantee to bring about any and every change in his patient's condition. I suggest that the playwright of *Mitleid*, working in the naturalistic mode, found a similar tenuousness in his own practice not entirely uncongenial. At the very least it provided him with a justification for confining his work to ante- and post-mortem analysis, to demonstrating, by means of exemplary cases, the reasons why his patients were in danger of expiring. As a diagnostician, Hauptmann became the pride of his profession; as a healer, his skill never went much beyond the administration of pain-killing injections or compassionate narcotics. Thus his recourse to *Mitleid*, however admirable in other respects, betrays a certain failure of nerve, a refusal to involve himself directly in the very issues he was professing to raise. His very moral play lacks a genuine moral stance: for morality, if it means anything at all, means acting upon the decisions one has made about how to cope with a real situation.

This judgment may be tempered somewhat by considering the enormous difficulties Hauptmann — or for that matter, the other playwrights of his generation — were up against. The subject can be handled simply, without ranging too far in historical background, by concentrating on the form in which Hauptmann cast his play. We have already quoted Kenneth Burke to the effect that one synonym for strategy was "stylization" and that the great literary forms provide a kind of equipment for living. Applied to *Einsame Menschen*, this observation requires us to explain the playwright's use of the naturalistic mode and his decision to structure the drama within the framework of ostensible tragedy. What is particularly significant here is Hauptmann's attempt to join poetic elements that many critics consider incompatible.

Hauptmann's gravitation to naturalism is easy to understand and some of the reasons for it have already been given earlier in this essay. What naturalism may have meant to him, however, is less well understood, as is the ex-

tent to which he shared some of the fundamental assumptions about it with other naturalists. The most superficial,
and therefore least useful definition (which unfortunately
is also the one most frequently cited) is that naturalism has a bias towards a certain kind of subject matter. A naturalistic play is supposed to depict actual social
or psychological misery with a maximum degree of objectivity, offering a slice of life that invariably turns out to be
on the mouldy side or has some incipient decay not immediately visible to the unsuspecting consumer. The German
naturalists were often reproached at the time for their interest in the sordid and ugly, or — forgive me for ham-
mering at this point — in the "unnatural," a predilection
that alienated many of their contemporaries and sparked
innumerable, not entirely worthless debates about the true
function of art. Hauptmann himself was accused in *Vor
Sonnenaufgang* of "carrying filth on to the stage in buck-
ets and turning the theatre into a cesspool." Meanwhile,
that respected Dean of the Old School, Ibsen's friend Paul
Heyse, tried to discount the naturalists' entire endeavor
with a pithy couplet in *Knüttelvers*:

> Die Muse wandelt in stolzer Ruh
> Vorbei und hält sich die Nase zu.[10]

Yet critics and appearances to the contrary, the naturalists
did not all enjoy wallowing in the mire nor did their prob-
ing of "filth" go very far. Compared to the so-called deca-
dents who immediately followed them in German literature, they were less interested in ugliness than they were
moved by misery; they were prompted less by fascination
than by repugnance. What most naturalists were trying to
do shows quite clearly in the fact that they invariably depicted a social abuse or evil as a *Verkehrtheit*, that is, as a

10. "The muse passes by in calm disdain, holding her nose." Cited in
Artur Kutscher, *Frank Wedekind: Sein Leben und seine Werke*, 1:141.

perversion or distortion, as something "turned away" from the conventionally true, something "wrong" for which there was a recognizable "right." Hence the analogy with medicine already noted in Hauptmann's case. Like him, most naturalists concentrated on exposing pathological conditions because they believed that an awareness of the sickness was a necessary precondition for eventually restoring the healthy or normal state. "Natural," then, has a double meaning in this transitional era: it reflects not only the preoccupation with actual or factual circumstances, with the prevailing state of human affairs, but also the preoccupation with man in his normal condition. The naturalists' truth involved both the nature of things as they are and the nature of things as they should be.

This notion of a two-sided truth is reflected, for example, in the naturalists' handling of scene and setting. The usual habitat of contemporary man, as they picture it, is an urban interior, a world of man-made things, characterized either by extreme deprivation or extreme luxury. Nature, on the other hand, the physical landscape and countryside, the entire organic world outside, figures primarily as a contrastive background. Following the example of Zola's *Thérèse Raquin*, nature in most naturalistic plays is banished from the stage, a reality existing only as a recollection of what the dramatis personae once knew or as a longing for something they will never experience. The point, of course, is that man has lost his contact with nature and become a prisoner of his environment or milieu; moreover, this loss is symbolic, if not necessarily determinative, of man's present condition and the changes in his own nature. So it is in Hauptmann. Even though he occasionally sets his scene outdoors or shows his characters briefly rejuvenated through exposure to the forces of nature, the irony of a double truth is merely confirmed by the contrast.

The significance of this from our point of view is that the naturalists *did* proceed on the basis of a standard or norm. Stated or not, the norm was always implicit in their descriptions, either as the positive face on the other side of life's negative coin, or more fundamentally, because it was taken for granted as belonging to the system of values which most naturalistic writers shared with their contemporaries. And this concept of "natural" in the positive sense was determined almost entirely by the social and moral order inherited from the nineteenth century, its values and ways of thinking, the entire "system of pieties," as Kenneth Burke might describe it, which gives a man "the sense of what is proper to what." [11] I do not mean to say the naturalists accepted everything their fathers bequeathed them lock, stock, and barrel. But they did tend to judge contemporary appearances by the only standards available to them, and any objections they raised were directed at imperfections in the system (rigidity, malfunction, hypocrisy) and not at the assumptions or principles which held that system together. Contrary to widespread impression, neither the naturalists nor Gerhart Hauptmann were very revolutionary minded, however their program or talk. Nietzsche's day had not quite dawned. It might be more accurate to speak of that generation as "inverted idealists" [12] or as uncertain romanticists, filled with anxiety and already nostalgic for the order that was soon to pass away. Even those who were bent on attacking the old institutions aimed at a utopia which, in effect, would be little more than the rerighting of a condition that most of them acknowledged as fundamentally good.

In sum, the naturalistic generation of writers, Haupt-

11. Kenneth Burke, *Permanence and Change*, p. 741f.
12. The term is applied by Irving Babbitt to the French realists, in *Rousseau and Romanticism*, p. 93.

mann again included, found themselves caught in a dilemma for which there was no apparent resolution.
Deeply attached to bourgeois values and unaccustomed to
disruption, they found it unthinkable to do away with the
old system of pieties even though it had let them down by
its inability to accommodate the new. At the same time,
they were uncertain that their once-reliable instrument of
change, rationalistic science, would continue to serve
them well. The forces and powers discovered by science
appeared increasingly beyond man's control and yet ever
more determinative of his condition. The more one
learned about the world, the less it seemed susceptible to
human influence. Faced with this dilemma — a truer one
than Johannes Vockerat's — the naturalistic generation
opted for a stylistic mode which allowed them to pay lip
service to the idea of change without forcing them to risk
defeat trying to face the issue head-on. The naturalistic
approach displayed their concern for actuality and their
ability to treat it objectively. At the same time, it demon-
strated, in a rational way, why any direct or immediate
measures would be futile. Their way out was to substitute
Mitleid for morality, the pathos of shared emotions for the
ethics of decision-making, with the result that they left
the present in its state of suspension between old and
new, between memory on one side and hope on the other,
both of them illusions sustained by the notion of a "natural" order of things as they should be. Naturalism, in
short, became that generation's mode of compromise.

The naturalistic approach, pretending to take things exactly as they were and yet taking only those things which
would lead to the formation of a desired attitude, inevitably led to irony. Occasionally, as in the work of Arno
Holz, to whom Hauptmann dedicated his first play, the
irony was involuntary; in Hauptmann, however, it was intended to support the general effect of his work. The dif-

ference in these two cases is enlightening and may be explained as resulting from the two men's willingness, or unwillingness, to tamper with their chosen mode. Arno Holz is responsible for one of the silliest definitions of art ever formulated in any language. All good students of German drama know it by heart: "Die Kunst hat die Tendenz, wieder die Natur zu sein" ("Art tends to be nature again").[13] Fortunately, few naturalists were deceived by the simple-mindedness of Holz's formula — how can art be something again which it never was nor ever shall be? — but the notions associated with his formula, the so-called theory of *konsequenter Naturalismus*, have done much to discredit the whole movement. Holz was undoubtedly more intelligent than his words suggest, and certainly he was the most innovative of all naturalists as far as technique is concerned, but he probably never realized, in collaborating with his friend Johannes Schlaf on *Die Familie Selicke* (*The Selicke Family*), that his unyielding devotion to the mode of compromise had resulted in a parody of drama (or is it a parody of life?) that ironically refutes the very theory on which it is based. The frame Hauptmann chose for his naturalistic play, on the other hand, casting the situation in terms of a dilemma, saved *Einsame Menschen* from parody but could not elevate it to genuine tragedy. Lacking is any sense of inevitability resulting from the interaction of character with character, or character with a situation that is at least partly of the hero's own making; missing, in fact, is any action at all, for the play only exposes a condition already in being and discloses the premises of its foregone conclusion. Johannes's predicament may be occasioned by circumstances, but it is not inherent in them. Its dilemmic nature, as even Anna Mahr perceived, only appears so be-

13. Arno Holz, "Kunsttheoretische Schriften," *Werke*, 5:16.

cause the man himself cannot measure his situation
rightly. Thus, when Johannes gives up, it is not because
he *has* to after a series of decisions which leave him no
other choice, but because the playwright wishes to employ these means for underscoring his character's long-
threatened moral collapse. Neither Hauptmann's protagonist nor the play's other characters profit from this ending:
there is no uplift, no glimpse of a spirit resurrected in
defeat, no understanding of the dimensions of a fate
which has uttered judgment against a valiant protester.
And of Aristotle's famous "through pity and fear effecting
the proper purgation of these emotions," whatever we
might understand by that, *Einsame Menschen* shows
barely a trace. Instead of tragic fear we have anxiety, instead of tragic pity we have pathos and compassion. The
situation is more ironic than tragic.

One might argue that Hauptmann's failure to create a
tragedy in the naturalistic mode — if indeed this was his
intention in *Einsame Menschen* — results from his having
misunderstood both concepts. The attempt, in other
words, was something like trying to pour new wine into
old bottles, with the predictable result that the vessel
broke and the liquid spilled. There may be another explanation. Tragedy, of course, expresses our sense of life as a
fateful course, inevitably leading to death, and it calls for
resignation to what must be. And we do resign ourselves,
because tragedy gives us a vision of the powers we are up
against and shows us how to accept our defeat with dig-
nity. Yet as we have seen, the situation in *Einsame
Menschen* does not satisfy these sublime requirements;
rather, the standards of tragedy are imposed on the material in the guise of an apparent dilemma. Is it not possible,
therefore, that Hauptmann's gravitation toward the tragic
was an attempt to ennoble a situation that was not inher-
ently worthy of the stance he assumes towards it? The im-

plications are grave, but in view of what has been said so far, it is difficult not to conclude that his choice of the tragic frame, like his choice of the naturalistic mode, arose from the necessity of justifying some compromise he had made with his own conscience. Thus, style betrays the man and strategy reveals a personal as well as a public situation.

3

The Strategy of Reformulation
Frank Wedekind's
Frühlingserwachen

THE SAME YEAR *Einsame Menschen* achieved official success on the German stage, Frank Wedekind's *Frühlingserwachen* (*Spring's Awakening*) appeared in book form in an obscure publishing house in Switzerland. Stylistically the very antithesis to Hauptmann's drama, the work found little response among the naturalists and its censurable matter made it impossible to risk a presentation on stage. For fifteen long years it remained unperformed and unhonored, until Max Reinhardt finally persuaded Germany to have a look at it. Yet this remarkable work is a more original play than *Einsame Menschen*; its strategy for meeting the problem of change is addressed specifically to the situation Wedekind creates in the play; and in rejecting the notion that reality is to be found in actuality, *Frühlingserwachen* begins that destruction of illusionistic theatre which has continued into our own time.

Mindful that in good drama the last things always determine the first, I shall begin by recalling the final scene. The setting is a graveyard. Into it stumbles young Melchior Gabor fleeing from the reform school to which his parents had sent him after discovering evidence of "exzeptionelle geistige Korruption."[1] He had drawn some pictures for a school chum to explain the sex act and later got fourteen-year-old Wendla Bergmann with child, which she lost, along with her own life, when her mother insisted on an abortion. An outcast and a murderer now, his pockets empty and his coat in tatters, Melchior is close to despair and ready to contemplate suicide. "So neiderfüllt ist noch kein Sterblicher über Gräber gewandelt."[2]

The melodrama of this scene soon becomes grotesque. Just as Melchior decides to tear himself away from the cemetery he spies his friend Moritz Stiefel coming across the graves, head tucked underneath his arm. Moritz had shot himself after failing his exams and has returned to invite Melchior to join him in death. "Gib mir die Hand,"[3] he invites repeatedly, arguing the advantages of a life beyond: rest instead of flight, satisfaction instead of uncertainty, invulnerability to suffering, and an "unnahbare Erhabenheit [. . .] tatsächlich der einzige Gesichtspunkt, unter dem der Quark sich verdauen läßt."[4] It's a weighty list of compensations, and Melchior is strongly disposed to accept it. But again a figure appears out of nowhere, this time an elegant gentleman in white tie and tails, top hat and dress cape, wearing a mask. "Der vermummte Herr" has come to argue in favor of life. He first forces Moritz to admit that his reasoning was sheer humbug and the invitation to Melchior was motivated by mere envy and loneliness; then he suggests that Melchior will forget his sickness of heart once he has had "a good warm supper in his belly." Finally, as a way of overcoming Melchior's feelings

1. "Extraordinary spiritual corruption."
2. "No mortal ever wandered over graves so enviously."
3. "Give me your hand."
4. "An unapproachable sublimity; as a matter of fact, that's the only angle from which you can stomach such a mess."

of guilt, he proposes that morality is, after all, only the product of imaginary factors. Melchior is persuaded. Bidding farewell to his friend, he stalks out over the graves into the future, while Moritz prepares to straighten up his tombstone and descend again into his little plot of earth. "Und wenn alles in Ordnung, leg' ich mich wieder auf den Rücken, wärme mich an der Verwesung, und lächle . . ." [5] The turning point in this scene is the Masked Gentleman's definition of morality. His exact words are: "Unter Moral verstehe ich das reelle Produkt zweier imaginärer Größen. Die imaginären Größen sind Sollen und Wollen. Das Produkt heißt Moral und läßt sich in seiner Realität nicht leugnen." [6] The boys are inclined to regard this formula as a kind of existential magic spell. Moritz wishes he had heard it before, since he feels that morality was responsible for causing him, literally as well as figuratively, to "lose his head," and Melchior claims that only morality would have been to blame had he given Moritz his hand. Both are wrong, according to the Masked Gentleman, for each had simply followed his own nature. Moritz, always the timid one, fearful of life and the results of living it, would have committed suicide in any case, whereas nothing could have quenched Melchior's irrepressible thirst for life and his eagerness to throw himself into it, regardless of the consequences. The Masked Gentleman's formula, then, is actually a rationalization, a way of dealing with difficulties that are bound to appear in the process of living, a way of justifying one's instinctive desire to risk life whatever it might bring.

5. "And when everything is put back to rights I'll lie down again on my back, warm myself on the putrefaction, and smile . . ."
6. "By morality I understand the real product of two imaginary factors. The imaginary factors are obligation and desire. The product is called morality and its reality cannot be denied."

Some admirers of this scene would have been happier had the Masked Gentleman's little formula been left out, for its epigrammatic tone jars among the lyrical-rhetorical notes elsewhere in the play, and the blunt talk about morality, if not downright inappropriate under the circumstances, still strikes one as somewhat overdone. How cynical of Wedekind to define morality with a neat turn of phrase and then offer it in all seriousness as a means of absolving a guilty conscience! It would be interesting to have observed the reactions of a contemporary audience to this scene, had it only been given a chance to view the play, but certainly it would have realized what is at stake here and squirmed visibly at the thought. For when Wedekind wrote *Frühlingserwachen*, the fact and implications of morality were still something to be reckoned with. Involved was no less than the ideology of a whole culture: its thoughts and rituals, its symbols of authority, the institutions guarding its values and the ethics controlling its behavior, the frame for experience and the touchstone of right action, the mother of all pieties and the indispensable sense of what properly goes with what — all this is morality when it still has teeth in it, and that's why Moritz blames it for his suicide and why Melchior pauses to weigh the doubtful values of life against the sure comforts of death. And this, as we know from our discussion of Hauptmann's play, was a central issue in the age of transition, the problem of how to get through life without giving up, how to experience change and absorb its consequences without rejecting moral standards completely or succumbing to the powerful system already existent.

It is important to clarify the situation for which the Masked Gentleman's formula was made. *Frühlingserwachen* deals with a group of very young people, most of them about fourteen, who are going through the disruptions of puberty and can find no way to handle their doubts and fears, either in their own limited experience or in the precepts of their parents and teachers. All of them have what society must call unnatural or perverted experiences — suicide, extramarital pregnancy and abortion, prostitution, homosexuality, relegation from home and school to a house of correction — a series of calamities which seem fully to justify Wedekind's subtitling the play a "children's tragedy." Now somehow, in the unwholesome way in which Anglo-Saxon understatement sometimes underleaps itself and falls in the muck, Wedekind's designation has come to mean for many people the tragedy of sex. Certainly there is plenty of this in *Frühlingserwachen*, but to hit upon sex as the core of the play is to strike a bit off target, for the play is not really about these things at all, but about puberty, that is, about a general human experience with varied manifestations, of which the deviant ways of the pubescent libido are simply the most obvious and the most unsettling.

The situational symbolism of puberty is clear. It is the passage from childhood into adulthood, when the undifferentiated youngster turns into the unique boy or girl; the watershed between innocence and knowing, when irresponsibility turns into moral accountability; the time for marking off a new generation from an old one, when a ward becomes a citizen of the community — an event still celebrated in some societies by an appropriate ritual; and that moment of life when transfers occur which are of the utmost consequence to the individual, to the generation, and to human life itself. In short, puberty is par excellence the symbol of transition, transition as a universal phenomenon of change — in physical and human nature, and, we surmise, in all the forms of history that man has had a hand in making.

Frühlingserwachen is no less direct about the essence of puberty. Above all, it is an eruption of nature. During it, such vital forces as the ability to understand and make decisions, or the power to create and procreate, thrust themselves into consciousness and demand an outlet for their potential. And because these forces are ambivalent, they are also full of danger. Subjected to changes he can never be completely prepared for, the youngster during puberty is unpredictable and uncertain, egocentric and extreme, at one moment too brash and in the next crushed with doubt or self-pity, unsure whether he wants to fulfill the promise others hold out for him or whether he should disown everything that has already been done in his name. To everyone but himself, and sometimes even to himself, the nature of pubescent nature seems at times fundamentally irrational and anarchic, threatening to revert at any moment to some horrendous and permanent aberration. Puberty, in short, is a generational baptism by fire. And exposed to that purgative light, the most natural desires sometimes take on a sickly pallor, and the urgings of nature assume distorted shapes. This, perhaps, is the initial, "realistic" motive for Wedekind's wide spectrum of sexual manifestations and abnormalities, a register, incidentally, that coincides remarkably with the famous categories even then being established by Freud as typical for all human behavior. Melchior is being sadistic when he strikes Wendla with a whip and arouses emotions that bring them together in the hayloft, while Wendla, who yearns for self-sacrifice and the experience of abuse, shows a masochistic streak in provoking and enjoying his maltreatment. Moritz's weird dream of a headless queen who awaits deliverance through a two-headed king reveals an incestuous-narcissistic search for complements in himself, while Ilse, the wondrous *Freudenmädchen* he is afraid to take when she offers herself, is a joyously exhibitionistic nymphomaniac for whom natural promiscuity has become a way of life. And then Hänschen Rilow, that strange and gentle boy who knows everything and seems to experience only negatives, leads the spectrum further into the shadows as he wends his independent way from autoeroticism to homosexuality.

Now Wedekind's purpose in exposing such aberrations, if we are to believe the literary histories, was to expose Victorian parental or educational attitudes towards sexual mores as a climate in which such shocking things are bound to happen. This view is based on the supposition that Wedekind was a moral reformer — a category, by the way, which was established for him rather late in his career by those well-wishers who hoped to hasten the day when he might become *salon-*, or at least *bühnenfähig*. I have no wish to quarrel with this point of view at the moment, except to remark that it seems to me to exclude a good deal of what the play is all about. Not sexual mores are at stake, but a situation in which one of life's fundamental transfers, the transition from childhood to adulthood, is accomplished only at the cost of serious distortion and perversion. The failure involves both the older generation, which has shown itself unable to assist in the transfer, and the younger generation, which has not been able to orient itself in the face of such cataclysmic change. The result is helplessness and demoralization all around, the whiplash of conscience and shame, and a general uncertainty about what is proper to what. Now this, I submit, is fundamentally the same crisis, written small, as that faced by most of Wedekind's contemporaries and so well represented in another way in Hauptmann's *Einsame Menschen*. Think again of Johannes Vockerat, that sorry victim of pieties so lacerated by conscience that he believes he has no other choice than to kill himself. Is it not possible that Wedekind, in writing *Frühlingserwachen*, was also thinking of the real-life predicament represented in Hauptmann's play? A conscious relationship between the two works is out of the question, of course, for Wedekind could not have known *Einsame Menschen* when he wrote his own play; the interesting fact is that *Frühlingserwachen,* in its own manner and with its own perceptions, also has something to say about the realities of historical transition through the metaphor of puberty. There is no doubt that both playwrights tried to base their work on real life. Hauptmann dedicated his drama to "those who have already lived it," and Wedekind claimed that his work was "made up of personal experience or the experiences of school chums . . . almost every scene corresponds to an actual happening." [7] But here the similarities end, for Wedekind sees the relationship between actual and real quite otherwise than Gerhart Hauptmann and uses these words with a different meaning. For him an actual happening does not connote an historical event or specific social circumstance, and no such documentary facts are included in his play — no allusions to current affairs; no references to familiar places, dates, or names; nothing to identify the action as taking place at a known time or in a certain locale. Nor is there any attempt to exemplify a recognizable situation from everyday life by accurately rendering speech or gesture or tangible things — in short, nothing that necessarily points to the contemporary scene. In all these respects, *Frühlingserwachen* is nonillusionistic.

Wedekind's initial strategic advantage, then, was in freeing his play from any *Zeitgebundenheit*; another was in elevating the "actual" into a universal aspect of experience, as a reality occurring throughout nature and inherent in the very structure of existence. Puberty *is* such a natural reality, and so are the sexual and other tendencies

7. Frank Wedekind, "Was ich mir dabei dachte," *Prosa, Dramen, Verse,* 1:942.

associated with it. A third strategic advantage follows logically, for since the manifestations of puberty are natural,
they provide in themselves the only justification for being
as they are. Almost alone among the German writers of
that generation, if we do not count Freud as a literary artist, Wedekind presents the aberrations of pubescent sexuality (as distinct from their social effects) as perfectly
normal in themselves, just various possibilities offered by
nature in a time of radical change. In Hauptmann's play,
as we saw it, the meaning of "natural" still bears the con-
notation of inherited norm, the values established by an
older way of life or a system of pieties not yet completely
replaced. In *Frühlingserwachen,* on the other hand, norm
and purpose are determined solely by nature herself, that
purpose being to carry out the process of change according to the individual's own inner need. And morality is to
be gauged by this kind of reality: things either do or do
not assist the fulfillment of vital potentialities, they either
do or do not lead to fruition.

In this connection, it is interesting to notice how Wedekind handles the effects of transition already observed
in Hauptmann's play. Human relationships, for example,
which are depicted in *Einsame Menschen* as problematic,
appear in *Frühlingserwachen* as non-encounters or as con-
tacts soon broken or unnaturally carried out. Moritz
misses his chance to know another human being and experience life when he turns down Ilse's easy proposition;
Wendla and Melchior are given no opportunity to develop
their relationship further and the child they conceive
is aborted; Hänschen Rilow, wearied by non-response
from his photographed courtesans, seeks temporary solace
in the arms of his friend Ernst Röbel. Their sterile exchange of kisses in an arbor teeming with ripe grapes is
surely one of the most touchingly ironic scenes in all German drama.

Similarly, the irrational, which appears in *Einsame Menschen* as an occasional effect without apparent cause, is a pervasive and immediate fact for Wedekind's youngsters; for them, nothing they feel quite fits the categories of what they already know or have been taught, and the things most important to their experience seem to elude reason entirely. Hauptmann's characters had balked in the face of the signs of the irrational; Wedekind's have to recognize it as the sole motivating force of change which willy-nilly will make its own outlets if none are provided for it.

The role of authority also undergoes permutation. Johannes Vockerat still believes in a law outside himself without being able to choose between alternatives; his indecision cuts him off from participating in change and makes him a victim of assertive pieties. In *Frühlingserwachen* there is no such confusion. Wedekind's youngsters no longer expect anything from the guardians of authority, for they have placed their questions and received no answers, either out of shame (on the part of their parents) or out of indifference (on the part of their teachers), and they know that no one will help them enter the adults' world. In *Einsame Menschen* it is the younger generation, however reluctantly, which seems to be breaking away from the older one; in Wedekind's play it is the other way round. Melchior is expelled for conveying information about the sex act and is sent by his own parents to a house of correction so that he will learn to "consult the law and not his own inclinations"; and feckless Moritz, so terrified by the thought of failure that he shoots himself, suffers the ultimate indignity of being rejected in death by his own father. Standing at the boy's graveside, Mr. Stiefel declares "in a voice choked with tears": "Der Junge war nicht von mir! Der Junge hat mir von kleinauf nicht gefallen!" [8]

Now since transition in puberty is a natural process, it can hardly be in itself the occasion for tragedy. Why then was Wedekind so preoccupied with showing the perversions of puberty and what justifies his calling *Frühlingserwachen* a "children's tragedy"? An answer to the first question is implicit in what has already been said about his passion for presenting things as they really are. In choosing puberty as his subject, Wedekind was simply being more perspicacious than most colleagues about "the real forces of existence" (his own terms), more radically honest than any in exploring its effects, and on firmest ground in viewing these from the standpoint provided by nature itself. What he meant by calling the play a tragedy — clearly, the term is not being used here in the technical generic sense — follows from our statement of the situation. Tragedy exists because the youngsters undergoing radical change are not provided with socially acceptable channels for their energies and the transfers normally occurring at puberty do not take place: instead of becoming part of the adult community the children are excluded or isolated from it; the things they should know are kept from them; and they lose their innocence without gaining compensatory values from the system of pieties. Perversion does exist in this world — not as manifestations of the libido, however, but as a frustration of the life-force and in the blockage of nature's purpose.

What then brings about such a "tragedy"? The power of morality, of course, or rather of an attitude toward it based on an exaggerated sense of piety and a false notion

8. "This boy wasn't mine! I didn't like what I saw in him from the very beginning!"

of what morality really is. Not the system is primarily at
fault, for it cannot help being what it is and cannot be dis-
pensed with, but the fear of transgressing the system; not
the existence of unexplained forces in one's self which
contradict the system, but lack of trust in one's capacity
for controlling them. The real enemy is conscience. All
this is summed up by the Masked Gentleman in providing
Melchior with a rationalization for continuing to live. Recall his curious statement that morality is "the real product of two imaginary factors." He gives no further explanation, and although the cemetery, as he points out, may
not be quite the place to carry out a long and profound
debate on the matter, we may still regret the casualness
with which he tosses off the remark. In any case we are
left a relatively free hand to interpret what he means. The
beginning of the Masked Gentleman's wisdom — or Wedekind's, if you like, since he dedicated the drama to this
figure and chose to play the role himself many times on
stage — lies in accepting the fact that morality is "real
and cannot be denied." It goes with living, is always with
one, and leaves one no choice but to reckon with it. It is
the inevitable concomitant of reality wherever human action is involved. The Masked Gentleman goes on to speak
of this reality as a "product," the result of an interaction
between two forces. It must then belong to a dynamic and
not a static order and cannot be embodied permanently in
a code or law or institution. Although universal itself, the
forms of morality are not absolute and are constantly subject to change. That product results, furthermore, from
factors which are "imaginary." Either this means the factors themselves are not objectively certain, but only as one
conceives them; or that they do not really exist and are
only apparent; or that they have only the value one as-
cribes to them arbitrarily according to the needs of the situation. Finally, the Masked Gentleman identifies these

imaginary factors as "desire" and "obligation," thereby reducing all the grand determinants of morality to a single
type of opposition: between what one wants to do as determined by nature (the volitional and the personal) and
what one ought to do as imposed by an external authority
(the abstract and the communal). In short, morality is not
at all, as the boys had thought, equatable with an inherited system of pieties; it is a universal reality arrived at in
individual instances by calculating the interaction of factors which themselves have only relative and arbitrary
value.

One need not agree with the Masked Gentleman, or
with this interpretation of what he says, to perceive what
is happening here. The existence of morality is left un-
challenged, but the terms used to describe it are being so
radically altered that the phenomenon itself is no longer
the same. Under the Masked Gentleman's formula the system of pieties loses its sanctity and symbols of authority
are stripped of their substance, while precept and law are
mocked for their claim to utter the last word on behavior
or to exercise the right of final judgment. The reformulation does not so much replace the tenets of morality as in-
fuse them with a new spirit. At the same time, the system
itself is relegated to an inferior place in the order of things
and its power nullified by simple refusal to acknowledge
its basic assumptions. Yet although the Masked Gentleman may be impious, he is not amoral; he is in fact an impious moralizer, supplanting "Morality," written large and
grounded in social institutions, with "morality," written
small and based on the "real forces" of nature, a natural
morality. Thus Wedekind points to that transvaluation of
values which is the ultimate purpose of any transitional
process.

The proof of the Masked Gentleman's formula lies in its
ability to make life seem worth living. For Melchior it is

the right phrase for the right man at the right moment and he accepts the rationalization as expert advice on how to encounter the uncertainties ahead. Nevertheless we have to admit that this "solution" does not really solve anything; it just restates the problem in terms that admit of an answer. Melchior does not tackle the difficulties inherent in his situation, he bypasses them; instead of removing an obstacle, he simply walks around it and continues on his way. As a cure for neurosis, the formula could hardly be improved, and as already implied, Wedekind may well have been thinking of the Johannes Vockerats around him when he devised the strategy for his play. A man does not get through an age of transition by worrying himself to distraction about the insurmountable problems of change, he accepts the fact as natural and inevitable, abandons what is no longer satisfactory, forgets about possible complications and justifies his course as best he may. Equipped with the Masked Gentleman's rationalization, no one need give up in despair. It is as valid for a Johannes Vockerat, who succumbs because he is afraid to say no to what has been or what no longer has validity for him, as it is for a Moritz Stiefel, who dies because he is afraid to say yes to what might be and take the consequences of his action. It is precisely because Melchior trusts his instinctual urge toward life that his way leads him across the graveyard instead of ending in it.

There is a striking similarity between Wedekind's strategy and the psychoanalytic techniques of Freud. This is probably not a matter of dependency — as far as I am aware, Wedekind was not acquainted with Freud at the time — but of sheer contemporaneity. Both men propose a way of salvation for the disoriented, supplying purpose and will where there was only despair, and the cure works by "dissolving the system of pieties lying at the roots of the patient's sorrows or bewilderment." It converts by

changing attitudes. What is involved in both instances is a
linguistic procedure: the reformulation of traditional concepts opens up a new perspective. To quote Kenneth
Burke again with respect to the Freudian technique, "a
new rationalization [is] offered to the patient in place of
an older one which had got him into difficulties." [9]

Does this not also help explain the aberrant sexual phenomena in *Frühlingserwachen*? Like Freud, Wedekind re-
formulates in the vocabulary of impiety, in irreverent and
denigrating terms which he knew would shock, thereby
deriving the cure from the nature of the disease, a kind of
homeopathy in reverse. If man is indeed capable by nature of perversity and if anarchy and irrationality are inherent in transition, then one need not fear these manifestations, need not nurse a guilty conscience about desires
which the old system of pieties considers outrageous and
shameful. And if these abnormalities are in fact not abnor-
mal, if every man is essentially perverse until accommoda-
tion makes him otherwise, then there is also no cause for
feeling guilty because of one's tendencies, no reason to accept defeat, no point in blocking the will for the sake of
someone else's peace of mind. The only practical and sen-
sible strategy is to let reason admit the irrational. Since it
is the nature of life to display the unfathomable vital
forces, then one's response should include the incalculable
in one's calculations.

Comfort is not the purpose of this strategy. Melchior is
warned that the way ahead will be rough and dangerous,
and that he will be assailed at times with "an enervating
doubt about everything," including life or the point of living. As the embodiment of what he preaches, the Masked
Gentleman well knows his own nature and wears his mask

9. *Terms for Order*, p. 56. From "Secular Conversion" (1935), originally in *Permanence and Change: An Anatomy of Purpose*.

with good reason, for blunt as he is about stripping a situation down to the facts, he is most reticent when it comes to his own countenance. The essence of life will remain a tantalizing mystery; there is no hope of arriving at certainty through the cause-and-effect route of the preceding century. Life — this much at least is certain — must be taken on faith: "Du lernst mich nicht kennen," as the Masked Gentleman puts it, "ohne dich mir anzuvertrauen." [10] Still, this is not a blind faith; Melchior is equipped with his elegant mentor's formula about morality and this was designed to help him cope with whatever he might meet. What he has received is a technique for living, a weapon for dealing with change and turning it to best self-advantage. Thus did Wedekind serve his time by helping it face the fears of the time; in an age that saw the development of *Realpolitik* he devised a dramatic form which might be called, with a bit of indulgence, *Realdichtung*. Whether he was inspired by Bismarck's practice is an open question; a more immediate and demonstrable source was the circus, for Wedekind admired nothing so much as the circus virtuoso, especially the acrobat or tightrope dancer for whom life and his profession were identical and the practice of them an art — the art of maintaining oneself in an always tricky and dangerous medium, surrounded by the incalculable and operating in seeming defiance of physical laws. The artiste is a man who has perfected a limited means for a limited end, replacing the useless power of reason with a rationalized technique for keeping him up in the air and minimizing the danger of falling.

Thus at that very moment in history when his contemporaries were proclaiming the need to revive art by putting it in the service of life, Wedekind was trying to meet

10. "You'll never get to know me without entrusting yourself to me."

the needs of life by deriving his cues from the performing arts. It was to be the twentieth-century way. So was his attitude toward existence, which turns away from the tragic view of reality — for him this was no longer a real possibility — to adopt a good-natured shrug of the shoulders in acknowledgement of the way things really are. Wedekind himself insists that *Frühlingserwachen* is full of humor — and if there seems in our minds to be more than a trace of the gallows in it, then surely because he knew that one's coming of age, the transition into adult life or into another phase of history, traverses the cemetery across both real and symbolic graves.

4

The Strategy of Exchange
Georg Kaiser's
Von morgens bis mitternachts

MORE THAN TWO DECADES after Hauptmann and Wedekind, but already anticipated in the latter's work, German
drama enters a new historical phase that we shall call the
age of anarchy.[1] Of the many strategies devised for coping
with the anarchic situation, I have selected Kaiser's *Von
morgens bis mitternachts*, not only because it dates from
about the middle of the period (it premiered in 1917 during wartime on the stage of the Kammerspiele in Munich); but also because it represents a turning point in Kaiser's work and leads to the type of strategy soon to be
developed by Bertolt Brecht.

The protagonist of this play is the conscientious and su-
perefficient cashier of a provincial bank, so engrossed in
the routine business of taking in and paying out money
that he scarcely notices his customers. One morning fate
steps up to the counter in female form, a lady who wants to

1. In designating this phase the age of anarchy I follow both Bernhard
Diebold, *Anarchie im Drama*, and Hermann Broch, *Die Schlafwandler*,
part 2 of the trilogy: "Esch oder die Anarchie," although each uses the
term in a specialized sense.

cash a letter of credit without the necessary documents and offers in their stead to leave her diamond bracelet as security. The bizarre suggestion, her perfume, her exotic and sensual appearance — she's an Italian of course — and the snide remarks of his colleagues mislead the cashier into thinking she is a swindler prepared to sell herself for money, and when her hand accidentally brushes against his, he is undone. Stealing sixty thousand marks from the pile in front of him, he runs off to find her and make his proposition. Unfortunately, it was all a mistake. The lady *is* a lady, a doting mother trying to get funds transferred from her bank in Florence so that her son, an art historian, will be able to purchase a newly discovered Cranach. A criminal now as well as a fool, the cashier flees from the lady's hotel room out into a wide open field covered with snow and pauses to take stock of his situation. "Am Morgen noch erprobter Beamter," he muses, "[. . .] Mittags ein durchtriebener Halunke." [2] It's a heady change and the cashier fully understands its possibilities, for crime has freed him from a routine existence and brought him his first chance to experience life. The problem, as he sees it, is to find values he has never known, values equal to what he has staked in absconding with the money. "Wo ist Ware, die man mit dem vollen Einsatz kauft?! Mit sechzig tausend — und dem ganzen Käufer mit Haut und Knochen?! —— Ihr müßt mir doch liefern —— ihr müßt doch Wert und Gegenwert in Einklang bringen!!!! [3] At that moment the sun hides behind a cloud and a sudden gust of wind whips his hat away, lodg-

2. "In the morning still a tried and true official [. . .] At midday, a cunning scoundrel."
3. "Where are the goods a man can buy by staking his all? With sixty thousand — and the whole purchaser with skin and bones? You [meaning the things of life] must let me have them — you must balance value with countervalue! ! ! !"

ing it in a nearby tree. As he goes to recover it, the cashier notices "handfuls of snow caught in its branches, forming a human skeleton with maliciously grinning jaws." This then seems to be his answer: death, presumably his own, will supply him with the values he seeks. It is not a very attractive suggestion, for having just bought his freedom at considerable cost the cashier is determined not to surrender life without first experiencing its "complications." Bidding a polite farewell to the apparition, and inviting it to call him again around midnight, the cashier departs to throw himself into the business of living.

The first part of *Von morgens bis mitternachts* ends with this decision; the second pictures the cashier's various attempts to balance value with counter-value in experience. He begins by returning home to make sure he has not overlooked anything of worth there. He hasn't, for this sphere of petty bourgeois domesticity — old mother at the window, daughters embroidering or playing Wagner, wife in the kitchen frying lamb chops — revolves around the same empty and unchanging routine as his existence at the bank. Having made sure that this world will not stand "rigid examination" or ever provide worthwhile experience, the cashier moves on to continue his search elsewhere. His next visit takes him to the world of sport and disinterested play, to a huge arena for marathon bicycle racing. Here, amid the motion, noise, and excitement, the cashier thinks for a moment he has discovered something of value — human beings no longer separated by self-interest but welded together in one great ball of elemental passion. Soon a prince enters the royal box, however, and the mob reveals its true character by falling into respectful silence. Disillusioned to find "dieser eben noch lodernde Brand ausgetreten von einem Lackstiefel am Bein

Seiner Hoheit,"[4] the cashier withdraws in scorn and disgust.

His way takes him next to the sphere of erotic and aesthetic pleasures, to a *separée* in a grand restaurant, where he seeks out a companion for the evening and waits for her to seduce him. But this *fille de joie* gulps down too much of his champagne and falls into a stupor. A second and third attempt are also frustrated: the masked beauties he has chosen for disrobing appear so ugly, in natura, he cannot bear to look at them, while the girl he selects to titillate him with dancing turns out to have a wooden leg. Having failed to make contact with a human being in this world of the flesh, the cashier leaves in desperation. (Ironically, although he leaves a large bill in payment, it is stolen before the waiter comes to get it.) His final stop is a mission of the Salvation Army, the sphere of organized religion. Sitting there in fascination while repentant sinners rise to deliver their testimony — sportsmen and prostitutes and a retired clerk, all of whom recapitulate his previous encounters — the cashier believes he has finally come upon something of value, a group of soulmates who have realized the futility of worldly pursuits and have elected to dedicate themselves to God and the salvation of their immortal souls. Persuaded to make his own confession, he tells the congregation that he has learned how money will not buy anything of value: "Mit keinem Geld aus allen Bankkassen der Welt kann man sich irgendwas von Wert kaufen. Man kauft immer weniger, als man bezahlt. Und je mehr man bezahlt, um so geringer wird die Ware. Das Geld verschlechtert den Wert. Das Geld verhüllt das Echte — das Geld ist der armseligste

4. "This conflagration, which was burning so brightly just a moment ago, put out by one of His Highness's boots."

Schwindel unter allem Betrug!"⁵ And acting on this conviction, the cashier tosses what is left of his sixty thousand marks out into the crowd. The effect is not quite what he anticipates, however, for as the banknotes fall in their midst, every one of the penitents leaps from the benches to scramble for his share and runs off with it into the night. A moment later the Salvation Army lass who had accompanied him to the altar with the promise to always stand by him appears with a policeman, denounces him as a thief, and demands the reward for turning him in. Suddenly the lights go out in the hall and, in the darkness, the glow of a street lamp shines through the window, "illuminating the arms of a chandelier so that they seem to form a human skeleton." It is the same death image which had appeared to the cashier earlier on the open field of snow. "Warum lief ich den Weg?" he cries. "Wohin laufe ich noch? [*Posaunenstöße*] Zuerst sitzt er da — knochennackt! Zuletzt sitzt er da — knochennackt! Von morgens bis mitternachts rase ich im Kreise — nun zeigt sein fingerhergewinktes Zeichen den Ausweg — — wohin?!!"⁶ He shoots himself to find the answer and falls "with outspread arms against a cross sewn on a curtain behind the altar."

Even this brief sketch of the action in *Von morgens bis mitternachts* makes it apparent that the world had changed radically when Kaiser wrote his play and that his view of reality differs significantly from Hauptmann's or

5. "You can't buy anything of value with money, even from all the banks of the world. You always get less than what you pay. And the more you pay, the less valuable the goods. Money decreases the value. Money covers up what's genuine. Money is the most miserable of all swindles!"
6. "Why did I take this way? Where am I still going? [*Trumpet blasts*] At the beginning he was sitting there — naked to the bone! From morn to midnight I've been running around madly in a circle — now a sign from his beckoning finger shows me the way out — — — where to? ! !"

Wedekind's. To review the new historical circumstances in detail is hardly necessary since our purpose here is neither to study the age nor to measure the playwright's accuracy in recording it, but to delineate (as Kaiser saw them) those fundamental developments which still offered man a possibility for moral choice. First of all, Kaiser has obviously rejected the notion that the best way to reveal reality is through the conscientious depiction of actuality. Although the play pulsates with the spirit of World War I Germany, nothing in it refers directly to historical circumstances, and none of its events or scenes or characters are meant to suggest actual counterparts in life. On the contrary, Kaiser has broken the frame of illusionism and thrown away the principles which held it together. Instead of verisimilitude we have improbabilities and distortions; instead of objective reportage, an arbitrary and obvious fiction; instead of a careful record of everyday speech, we get a flood of rhetoric. Nothing reveals this new dramaturgy more graphically, perhaps, than Kaiser's boldness in depicting the undepictable — the ultimate reality of death. Hauptmann's phenomenal world of things did not allow him to bring death on stage; Wedekind broke through this restriction by exhibiting death or the dead corporeally in their natural setting in the cemetery; Kaiser, unrestrained by any consideration except his symbolic purpose, conjures up death at will in a shape and form devised solely by imagination. The playwright's manipulating hand is everywhere visible in *Von morgens bis mitternachts*, flaunting his virtuosity, insisting that the play is sheer artifice and that only artifice makes the game worthwhile.

Like many early Kaiser plays, this one complicates its presentation of situation and strategy by elaborate linguistic conceits and blatant theatrical effects. Too much never seems enough in Kaiser's opinion, and where other playwrights are content to disarm their audiences with sporadic shocks, he discharges a constant barrage of words, images, sights, scenes, noises, and colors in a tempo rapid enough to send most spectators reeling. The meaning in the mélange usually clusters around a key metaphor — in *Von morgens bis mitternachts* it is the metaphor of money, chosen because it stands ambivalently for a real as well as a symbolic medium of exchange and also because of the opportunities it offers for punning on the problems of value. Following his own formula — "ein Drama schreiben heißt einen Gedanken zu Ende denken"[7] — Kaiser wittily traces a parallel set of implications in the metaphor, placing one in counterpoint to the other until a new perspective on both eventually emerges. Hence the ever present contrast between material and spiritual "goods," and the strong hints throughout the play that the cashier's real goal is his salvation through the *imitatio Christi.* Just before tossing his money to the crowd, he refers to the various steps in his search as *Stationen,* a clear echo of the Christian stations of the cross, and Kaiser supports this suggestion by his staging of the cashier's death. As he dies, he is made to fall "with arms stretched out wide" against a cross sewn on a curtain behind the altar. And just in case anyone might still miss the point, Kaiser adds in a stage direction: "Sein Ächzen hüstelt wie eine Ecce — sein Hauchen surrt wie ein Homo."[8]

The intent of all this seems obvious enough, and in fact most interpretations of *Von morgens bis mitternachts* differ in only minor respects. As one critic words it, the play is concerned with "the existential buying power of money," asking "whether it is possible with money to ac-

7. "Writing a drama means thinking a thought through to the end." "Der Mensch im Tunnel," *Das Kunstblatt* 6 (1922).
8. "His groaning rattles like an *ecce*; his breathing gasps like a *homo*."

quire the essence of life." [9] The answer, of course, is that money has no such power, and the cashier reacts to this insight by rejecting his materialist orientation for a spiritual (or is it an other-worldly?) one, thereby setting an example for us all to follow. He becomes, in effect, another embodiment of Kaiser's much-lauded Vision of the New Man (*der neue Mensch*), a self-sacrificing martyr for humanity.

Now it would be difficult to quarrel with this interpretation. It accords with most of the evidence and provides the play with a social-moral message corresponding to Kaiser's own brief against the predominantly money-oriented society of his day. Still, as a statement of situation and strategy, the interpretation sounds a bit simplistic, and I for one am reluctant to believe that Kaiser would have constructed such an elaborate work only to demonstrate a truism. Further doubts arise in reflecting on the link between the cashier's conscious search for value and his unconscious need to save his soul. Most interpretations accept this connection as "inspirational" rather than "logical," thereby sparing it further (and possibly damaging) scrutiny. Yet can we really take the cashier's search as a secular version of Christ's passion and crucifixion? If so, then why do Kaiser's parallels diverge more often than they coincide? On the other hand, if this notion is rejected, how are we to understand the playwright's cryptic *ecce homo*? Does the cashier stand for Everyman, as most critics seem to assume, or is he a unique and very singular martyr? And if a martyr, in what sense, for what values does he sacrifice himself, and how can these be recommended seriously to those who are still among the living?

Questions like these have been left unanswered; indeed,

9. Walther Huder, Postscript to his edition of *Von morgens bis mitternachts*, p. 70.

they are not usually even raised—perhaps because the
message is deemed moral enough to justify treating them
as irrelevant, perhaps because the impression still persists
that this *Denkspieler*, as Bernhard Diebold called
Kaiser,[10] is just frivolously playing with an idea instead of
thinking it through to the end. Be that as it may, I suspect
that the questions might not exist if the interpretation of
the play were of a different sort. My own feeling is that
Kaiser did not write *Von morgens bis mitternachts* simply
to propound an exemplary moral or social message; on the
contrary, I believe that his burden here was primarily
personal—conditioned by historical circumstances, to be
sure, and even arising in part from them, but ultimately
distinct and independent—and that the strategy he devised was intended to release him from that burden symbolically without exposing its nature to others. I propose
therefore to take a slightly different approach in this
essay, looking for an underlying personal situation, and in
so doing, to suggest how the terms employed so far may
be used to interrelate the personal and the historical dimension. The aim is not to point out facts of Kaiser's biography, but to analyze the way in which a peculiarly personal problem arises from his awareness of the times, and
how he attempts to transcend that problem in terms that
would also have significance for his contemporaries.

The action of *Von morgens bis mitternachts* proceeds
through three dramatic "acts" or stages—a before, a during, and an after—each of which represents a different
phase in the protagonist's development. The cashier
comes from the bank world, goes through various spheres
of mundane experience, and arrives at the negation of his
previous existence, with the transition between each of

10. See "Georg Kaiser der Denkspieler," *Anarchie im Drama*, pp. 363–
417.

these stages marked by his rejection of a previous role and his assumption of a new one. This is why his first transition, from bank to mundane world, is described in terms of death and rebirth; and this is also the significance of his suicide, by which the second transition is accomplished. Suicide, of course, is a symbolic way of indicating rejection of a past (or present) orientation in preparation for a new one. Put this way, the action refers not only to the cashier's search for value but also to the playwright's quest for identity; it is in fact a symbolic reenactment of Kaiser's own attempt to form a meaningful role for himself within the contemporary order of things. And this quest for identity is consubstantial with the formation of role — or transformation of role, as Burke points out — since the discovery of identity proceeds by various steps to the determination of one's true nature and function; one becomes " 'most thoroughly and efficiently himself' " by sloughing off "ingredients that are irrelevant to this purpose." [11] The process is "tragic" inasmuch as it requires a sacrifice of the self, or a part of the self, in order to transcend the unwanted condition (the cashier becomes the playwright's scapegoat); and in this particular case the process is essentially paradoxical as well since it concludes with the realization that the way up leads down (the usual route for martyrs), and that knowledge of one's role is gained only at the cost of losing one's illusions.

How is all this revealed in the play? The first stage of the action, I said, is a "before"-condition describing the cashier's situation while still in the bank world. We might call it a perverted state of innocence, for in this morally neutral state the cashier is without purpose or awareness and unthinkingly accepts the forms in which existence is presented to him, unwilling or unable to make decisions

11. Kenneth Burke, *The Philosophy of Literary Form*, p. 33.

about his own life. Here Kaiser describes the outward characteristics of historical reality in the first two decades of the century, and since his treatment of that reality is rather scanty in the play, it should be fleshed out somewhat in order to underscore the radical nature of the cashier's first change of role and also to review some of the developments that had taken place since Hauptmann and Wedekind had written their plays.

One notable development concerns the attitude towards change and its effects. In the first phase of German drama, you recall, men were keenly aware that they were living in a time of transition. Circumstances were being altered everywhere, everything was undergoing permutation, the facts of change were overwhelming, and the course of history appeared to follow a strictly linear evolution. The transitional generation's reaction to this situation was largely negative, in part because developments seemed to be determined by circumstances which no one could control, in part because time had not yet settled what would remain of the old order or what forms might be assumed by the new. The result was uncertainty and discomfort — disorientation and demoralization for the fainthearted creature of pieties, isolation and rootlessness for anyone bold enough to break with the past and strike out on his own. Both Hauptmann and Wedekind dealt with the critical problem of how to ride out the winds of change without being swept completely off course. Yet their reactions differed greatly, for as we saw, Hauptmann, electing to stress the "dilemmic" nature of the situation, called for a "tragic" resignation; while Wedekind, as if in response to this stance, drew upon an analogy with the processes of nature in order to emphasize that change was taking place in all forms of existence, social and moral as well as physical. He welcomed it, therefore, realizing that the viability of these forms lay precisely in their ability to undergo continual modification.

Historical developments after the turn of the century made the transitionist's evolutionary or linear view of change seem insufficient. In *Von morgens bis mitternachts* time seems to revolve in a circle, its changes nothing more than a recurrent and regular series of events, each discrete yet exactly like all the others, one moment simply exchanged for the next. Life has become routine in this world, an operation measured by clock and calendar and daily schedule, by the opening and closing hours of business, or by the needs of a system whose sole end is self-perpetuation. We observe the cashier going through the motions of such "change" at the bank; later we see him at home, in the bourgeois sphere Kaiser knew from his own background, where habit determines every move — "Morgens Kaffee, mittags Koteletts. Schlafkammer — Betten, hinein — hinaus" [12] — and nothing will ever be altered until death interrupts the cycle. The point is driven home melodramatically when the cashier's ancient mother, learning that her son will not eat the noonday meal with them as is his custom, collapses in her chair and dies of shock. The problem of change in this first part of the play, therefore, seems to be not how to go on living in spite of change, but how to recapture the sense of life which only experience, and experience of *different* things, can bring.

That problem was complicated by other historical developments. The fragmentation of human personality, for example, had degenerated by this time into pervasive dehumanization. At the beginning of *Von morgens bis mitternachts*, the cashier seems little more than the caricature of a human being, reduced by function and routine to au-

12. "Mornings, coffee; noon, cutlets. Bedrooms — bed, in — out."

tomatonic anonymity. His counterpart in social history was the *Kleinbürger*: clerk, minor bureaucrat, or secretary, the *functionary* who makes the wheels go around, eight to five in the office with an hour off for lunch, his only reward the pride of having performed with maximum efficiency. The cashier also goes about his work like a robot, never looking up from the pile in front of him, never addressing his clients or colleagues, only rapping on the counter occasionally when a transaction fails to run smoothly, apparently totally unaware of anything besides his counting, totally lacking in self-consciousness, totally without individual traits, a half-creature, a non-personality.

Similarly, human relationships — which Hauptmann pictured as problematic and Wedekind as frustrated non-encounters — appear in Kaiser's play as a set of empty and abstract forms. To his family, the cashier is merely Son, Father, Husband according to the social typology which marks his connection with them; to his co-workers at the bank he is just "the cashier," another employee. Neither love, collegial ties, nor bonds of friendship exist in this world. The only contact between human beings is functional.

The status of authority and the relationship of the individual to it had also changed. In the transitional period, the traditional forms of authority, manifested in bourgeois morality and supported by a lingering belief in deity, could still command allegiance in spite of their weakening position. Hauptmann's Johannes is defeated because he cannot shake off the forces of piety in himself; Wedekind's Melchior overcomes that force only by placing himself outside society and electing to act on his own. By the time of *Von morgens bis mitternachts*, however, most traditional forms of piety had collapsed, and the very possibility of a central or final authority had been abandoned. In

place of a single *Instanz* the world had split into multiple
sectarian factions, each asserting a claim to decide for all
the rest. Like the factory in Kaiser's *Gas,* the bank in this
play is a law unto itself, extending its power into the do-
main of human affairs as well as over technological
spheres. Supported by rationalized procedures and a comprehensive terminological structure organized around the
symbol of money, the bank stands as a miniature sphere of
the absolute, completely rationalized to ensure its func-
tioning with near-mechanical perfection. Everything in
this world is used for some limited purpose determined
by the overall needs of the system. And this impersonal
authority — the very thing the cashier deals with is an impersonal medium of exchange — has only an impersonal
relationship to those who service it. This is why the protagonist of Kaiser's play has no name, just a designation to
indicate his specific job within the organization: *Kassierer.*
Not even "*the* cashier," actually, but simply Kassierer, man
reduced to a means, the functional part of him standing
for the whole. In a fundamental sense, then, Kassierer
is without an identity, for there is nothing to which he belongs and nothing with which he can identify. Although
the bank supplies him with a livelihood, he is actually
alienated from it, not only materially in the sense of being
deprived of its goods and profits, but spiritually as well,
since he does not share in its rationale or purpose.[13]

This then is the "before" or initial stage of the action in
Von morgens bis mitternachts, a state of unselfconscious-
ness which would seem to preclude a man's ever becoming aware of his situation or taking the necessary
measures to break the circle of repetitions and undertake
a search for identity. But as usual in Kaiser's work, that
possibility is provided by the operation of chance, by an

13. Kenneth Burke, *Attitudes towards History,* p. 216.

entirely unforeseen and fortuitous event — in this play, by
the lady's unexpected appearance and the accidental
touch of her hand on the cashier's. Historically, this way
of motivating the action through happenstance suggests a
reawakened sense of the incalculable in human affairs
after decades of submitting to a cause-and-effect determinism. Wedekind too had acknowledged the incalculable, but always as a threat to the individual's moral
equilibrium; hence his strategic insistence on perfecting
rationalized techniques for survival. Kaiser, on the other
hand, regards chance as the giver of opportunities. Although neutral itself, its sources unfathomable and its results unpredictable, it has the incomparable advantage of
making one aware of possibilities and of opening up pros-
pects never perceived before, of giving man a choice.
Thus chance, as *accident*, becomes chance as *opportunity* — man's chance to effect his own salvation or discover
his true identity. We might think of it as a latter-day secular substitute for the supernatural act of grace, wholly appropriate in an era when men had become non-naturalists
as well as non-believers and had grown ever more cog-
nizant of the coexistence of irrational alongside rational
powers.

The accident which sets the action going in *Von morgens bis mitternachts* is slight but telling. What could be
more fitting (or what more devastating) for Kassierer
than the touch of a lady's perfumed hand? It is the first
unpremeditated event in his rationalized world, the first intrusion of an arbitrary and personal element into the
routine impersonality of his existence, his first genuine
"contact" with another human being. And the results are
electric. According to the playwright's ubiquitous stage
directions, couched in the amusing telegraphic style he
often uses in this period, Kassierer "dreht sich über die
Hand in seiner Hand [. . .] Büsche des Bartes wogen —

Brille sinkt in blühende Höhlen eröffneter Augen."[14] Obviously, he has been shaken to the roots of his being. Having never even looked at a client before, Kassierer now focuses on the exotic creature in front of him, seeing in her a whole universe of possibilities and sensing the hope and longing to experience them for himself. The lady, in short, has touched him with desire. And desire means purpose — the redirection of activity toward some goal of his own choosing or toward some accomplishment that will charge his life with meaning. Kassierer does not pause to consider what he is doing when he steals the sixty thousand marks and runs after his destiny, but clearly he is rejecting his previous role, a mere medium through which others are able to exchange one kind of value for another, in favor of a more active role, in which he can use the means now at his disposal to secure some of the goods of life for himself.

With choice, the process of rebirth becomes possible, and Kassierer sets out on his long and hectic search for value, the morning-to-midnight course by which he moves from one beginning to that even more radical beginning signified by death. His goal is determined solely by the lady and what she implies to him — something exotic and alien, anything and everything he has not known previously; reaction dictates his action. Instead of remaining in the bank world, then, where security is fixed and events predictable, Kassierer throws himself into a world of vicissitudes and uncertainty in the expectation of experiencing life through the accidents of fortune and of realizing change through their infinite variety. All the characteristics of the bank world, or of his position in it, are to be supplanted by their antitheses. The tried and true official turns into a "cunning scoundrel," an outlaw rejecting out-

---

14. "Bends over the hand in his hand [. . .] Bushes of beard sway — glasses sink into the gleaming cavities of eyes opened wide."

side authority in order to decide on his own, free from arbitrary regulations, free to set his own rules for the game and play it according to newly acquired wit and ingenuity. Rationalized organization gives way now to irrational caprice. Kassierer, acting as the impulse strikes him and at places and moments of his own choosing, invariably chooses the sensational and emotional, "letzte Ballungen in allen Dingen,"[15] a sensuous world of immediacy in which men and women are carried away by passion and ready to give their utmost for a "fabulous achievement." Taking another cue from the lady, Kassierer wants close physical contact in place of abstract relationships — in sport, in the dance, in sex, in all the bodily pleasures by means of which people try to forget their separate existences and do away with the artificial distinctions that keep them from knowing each other. Kassierer also discards his name in favor of an incognito, so that instead of being bound by a designation he will have maximum flexibility to assert his individuality and to assume an identity when the moment is opportune. He is able then to play a variety of roles throughout his search, as wealthy donor and sports lover, as playboy and man-about-town, as Master in search of a Mistress — whatever circumstances seem to require. The gamut of roles in this first part of the play is anticipated symbolically in that brief scene at home where Kassierer puts on smoking jacket, embroidered housecap, pipe and slippers, his usual domestic habit, only to remove them a few moments later and reclothe himself in garments more suitable for facing the great world outside. In sum, Kassierer forsakes a too-ordered world which now seems to him fatally damaging to human nature and turns to the opposite state of disor-

15. "Extreme concentration of effect in all things."

der, hoping to find value and purpose for his own existence in the realm of subjective experience and irrational drives. Significantly, Kassierer believes that the changes themselves signify a genuine rebirth. He reports to his uncomprehending wife that he has just come "from the cemetery [. . .] out of the grave" after digging his way free from the "mountains of debris" that had been heaped upon him by his years at the bank. "Es hat besondere Anstrengungen gekostet, um durchzukommen. Ganz besondere Anstrengungen. Ich habe mir die Finger etwas beschmutzt. Man muß lange Finger machen, um hinauszugreifen. Man liegt tief gebettet."[16] Although the effort has required him to dirty his fingers — we shall return to the pun — Kassierer does not feel impeded by what he has done and has no thought of repenting or turning back. On the open field of snow, anticipating Thomas Mann's more celebrated use of the element a few years later in *Der Zauberberg* (*The Magic Mountain*), Kassierer affirms his commitment to the course already begun and wipes out all traces of his background. Speaking of the snow skeleton but obviously meaning himself, he tells his wife: "[. . .] mein Gebein saß nackt. Knochen — gebleicht in Minuten. Schädelstätte! Zuletzt schmolz mich die Sonne wieder zusammen. Dermaßen von Grund auf geschah die Erneuerung."[17] So stripped of all encumbrances down to the bare essentials, Kassierer believes himself saved from nonentity, ready to experience life now as a new man.

Yet Kassierer, as it turns out, is wrong, for this supposed rebirth only makes his quest possible; it does not bring

16. "It took a special effort to get through. A very special effort. My fingers have gotten slightly dirty. It's necessary to dirty one's fingers to reach outside. One lies bedded a long way down."
17. "[. . .] my bones were naked — deathly pale within minutes. Place of the skull! In the end the sun melted me together again. This is how it happened, a complete rejuvenation."

him the values he seeks nor does it disclose the identity which is his final goal. It changes the circumstances of his life, to be sure, but not his basic orientation, and might even be considered a false course, in' that it leads him temporarily in the wrong direction. Kassierer is actually warned twice about acting on this assumption. The lady's rejection of his advances, for example, is clear evidence that some goods in life cannot be bought; belonging — that is, the possibility of identification — cannot be coerced. Kassierer ignores the hint, however. He assumes that the lady's rebuff has been forced on her. After all, the mother of a grown son might well have legitimate reasons for not wanting to enter into such a transaction. Moreover, he fails to perceive a difference between her motives and his own. The lady wants money — her own money! — out of an unselfish desire to assist her son in his work; Kassierer wants the lady in order to satisfy his own lust, or curiosity about it, regarding her as an object which can be acquired through means that do not belong to him in the first place.

The skeletal figure formed out of snow also warns Kassierer that he is going astray. Clearly, this image signifies that the kind of value Kassierer is searching for will be found only in negation: not in acquisition but in surrender; not in the flesh but in the spirit; not in some-thing, but in no-thing. Furthermore, when Kassierer recognizes that this image is already within him — "Ich glaube sogar, du steckst in mir drin"[18] — he should also realize that negation will require a symbolic sacrifice of his own self. The beginning of life, then, is to coincide with the termination of existence; the goal for Kassierer will be an end that has both literal and figurative meaning, which will stand for his objective as well as his means.

18. "I even think you are actually inside me."

Kassierer's "rebirth" is, then, much less and yet much more than he thinks: much more because it prefigures the realization at which he will eventually arrive; much less because he has, at this point, merely supplanted one set of externals for another — sets which are actually counterparts of each other. Through experience, he is soon to learn that order and disorder, authority and license, the limited sphere of rationalization and the unlimited one of irrationality are all merely complementary aspects of the same general anarchic condition. This first change in Kassierer's situation is not a genuine *conversion*, therefore, but simply an alteration of circumstances. It gives him an opportunity to deal with reality from its other side but will not itself make his life more meaningful. The "new" man, moreover, has much of the "old" Kassierer about him, for his conduct in the mundane world of experience is guided by the same principle with which he worked in the bank world. It is the law of a material quid pro quo: value gained must be equal to value risked, funds withdrawn matched by funds deposited, output equivalent to input, profits balanced against losses. Whatever the experience and whichever the sphere, Kassierer insists on matching *Wert* (his stake in existence) with *Gegenwert* (what existence will give him in return). And along with this tit-for-tat philosophy, Kassierer operates by that law of the marketplace according to which goods become the property of the highest bidder. At the sports arena, and later again at the great palace of pleasure, he continually raises his ante for the "goods" available in each sphere, hoping to secure the maximum value, assuming in good capitalistic fashion that quantity is proportional to quality and that the expenditure of "more" guarantees the acquisition of "better." Kassierer's mode of thought and action, then, like his vocabulary, still reflects the operational principles of the system he had presumably rejected.

So much for Kassierer's initial confusion with respect to means and ends. He now has a consciousness of purpose, thanks to the lady's appearance, but he has misunderstood (and therefore corrupted) its true nature by interpreting it according to the laws of the bank world. Not only does he assume an equivalence between material and spiritual values, he misjudges their nature as "buying" or "purchasable" powers. His is a classic instance of what Burke, borrowing a concept from Thorstein Veblen, calls victimization by "trained incapacity": that is, Kassierer has been so much a part of the bank world and so efficient in carrying out its tasks that his "very abilities function as blindness" when he faces a different situation.[19] The power of habit extends even to the way in which Kassierer continues to handle money in his "new" circumstances. When propositioning the lady, for example, he "breaks open a roll of gold coins, counts the pieces with professional expertise into the palm of his hand, then places them before her on the table." With this strong orientation to his former way of life, then, Kassierer can hardly be expected to undertake any action without perpetuating the cycle of errors linked to his past. Only his death, the complete erasure of what he was and what he belonged to, might make it possible for him to reorient himself and discover his true identity.

Kassierer's suicide is not only a repudiation of the past and an admission of guilt with respect to his errant way, it is also a punishment the author inflicts on himself that is integral to his strategy for coping with the burden laid upon him by the anarchic situation. Thus the playwright expiates his own sin with his protagonist's death; and, inasmuch as it represents a sacrifice of the self, or a part of

19. Kenneth Burke, *Permanence and Change: An Anatomy of Purpose*, pp. 7f.

the self, for something else, it becomes an act of propitiation too.

The root of Kassierer's guilt lies in his motivation, in his mistaking the opportunity chance has brought him in the person of the lady. As we know, her presence awakens desire and introduces a sense of purpose into a life previously without consciousness. This is a momentous event, yet Kassierer reacts to it with undue haste, drawing an unwarranted conclusion from appearances without pausing to reflect on the meaning of his choice. Prompted by deprivation and the casual remarks of his colleagues, he misinterprets the accidental touch of her hand on his as a "come-on" and misreads her offer to pawn the bracelet as a pledge of her own person. He sees only what she can bring him; he does not perceive what she is pointing to. Thus, in taking the lady for a swindler, he actually mistakes the whole situation: mistakes her identity, his own role with respect to her, and the significance of their encounter. Heedlessly, he sets his goal as the possession of values suggested by her presence and persists in pursuing this even after he learns that the goal is unobtainable and after he has been warned twice that it obscures a more fundamental possible purpose. Just as heedlessly, he grasps for means that are immediately at hand without considering whether or not these are the appropriate ones for realizing such an end.

Kassierer's guilt shows up symbolically in his embezzlement of the bank's funds. The implications of his stealing *money* will concern us in a moment; the fact that he *steals* money in order to strike out on his own reveals a psychological, or spiritual, guilt and indicates how we are to regard his subsequent actions. Crime, as Burke suggests, is the desperate gesture of the alienated man trying to belong somewhere to somebody or to achieve a sense of his own importance. It puts him in the center of things and links him — if only negatively, through his being "wanted" or pursued — with the rest of society. Everything a criminal does, everything that happens to him, is charged with meaning by virtue of its direct bearing on himself. In an impersonal or "determined" world, one apparently without purpose or value, crime restores the teleological point of view.[20] Whether or not Kaiser was aware of these particular implications is not important; the telling fact is that he chose to launch Kassierer into experience with a *crime* and that the crime he selected was embezzlement or theft. What Kassierer — or let us say outright, Kaiser — has made himself guilty of, therefore, is the fraudulent use of something entrusted to him as if he had the right to dispose of it according to his own wishes. The "mis-take" is literally that: the misappropriation of property that does not belong to him and is not proper for him to own or to use. It is also a fraud in that he pretends to be the possessor of means that are not rightfully his to employ.

But Kassierer steals money, of course, and money means power — the power to force results or control reactions as one sees fit. It is a primary instrument for satisfying desire. And power is indeed what Kassierer believes he has acquired in stealing the bank's funds. Initially, in approaching the lady, and subsequently in all the spheres of mundane experience, his invariable aim is to manipulate these means for mastering the situation and directing its outcome to his own wishes. In every instance his real purpose, rationalized as value, is to secure gratification where none had existed for him previously, either by imposing his will on others or by controlling the course of events to his own liking. His aim is not to experience the world's

20. See the discussion in Kenneth Burke, *A Grammar of Motives*, pp. 307ff.

pleasures himself — to share them with others or even
enjoy them vicariously — but to demonstrate his power to
determine the range, nature, or direction of what he wants
from others. It is the criminal's teleology. Thus he becomes a manipulator of passions and effects, deriving his
enjoyment in the sports arena from lashing the crowd
into a frenzy of excitement, in the palace of pleasure from
tempting the soubrettes to surrender their secrets and
throw themselves at his feet, and even in the Salvation
Army Mission from trying to persuade the down-and-out-
ers to follow his example in rejecting money as a source of
genuine values.

What is Kaiser trying to reveal (or, simultaneously, conceal) through his protagonist's theft of power? We have
said that the play is a quest for identity. Its action, then, is
a projection of what Kaiser imagined as a possible pattern
in his own life and the crime a symbolic way of pointing
to some crucial "sin," either one already committed or
simply one foreseen as a potential temptation and threat.
Not enough is known about Kaiser's biography to state
anything with certainty, but analysis of the play so far has
yielded some telling evidence. It seems obvious that Kassierer's original situation stands for the artist's alienated
predicament in a rationalized, money oriented society
where he is merely used and does not "count" for anything. Similarly, the various stages of Kassierer's search
correspond to the playwright's abortive attempts to assert
an identity by forcing the world to accept him on his own
terms. We can guess, furthermore, that the dimensions in
which he tries to exercise power are erotic, social, and artistic (or any combination of these), for each falls within
the conventional symbolic range of money and each is interwoven with the others in the overall texture of the
play's imagery. Very interesting is the fact that these dimensions are alike in that each is made up of individual,

"opposite" elements which, precisely by virtue of their being opposites, contain a potential for creativity. All this seems to be symbolized in the Cranach painting. It is, you recall, the cause of the lady's visit and of her subsequent encounter with Kassierer. He glimpses it briefly during his interview with her in the hotel room, and the vision of what he has seen returns to haunt him in the moments before he commits suicide. The attention Kaiser lavishes on this work of art suggests it may reveal something significant about the goal or motivating force of his play.

The painting has a conventional motif — Adam and Eve in the Garden of Eden — but according to the lady's enthusiastic son, Cranach's "remarkable treatment" of the subject is altogether unique. "Wir haben hier zweifellos die erste und einzige erotische Figuration des ersten Menschenpaares. Hier liegt noch der Apfel im Gras — aus dem unsäglichen Laubgrün lugt die Schlange — der Vorgang spielt sich also im Paradies selbst ab und nicht nach der Verstoßung. Das ist der wirkliche Sündenfall! [. . .] Hier jubelt zum erstenmal die selige Menschheitsverkündung auf: sie liebten sich!"[21] Paradise, then, is depicted as a state in which male and female are already together, knowing and being known by each other, their union an anticipation of the human community and a proclamation of mankind's future blessedness. The art historian goes on to point out how this ideal is realized structurally in the painting through the interaction of opposing forces: complete control in the midst of ecstasy, the meeting of horizontal and oblique planes, the straight line formed by the man's arm intersecting

21. "Here, without a doubt, we have the first and only erotic representation of the first human couple. The apple is still lying here in the grass — the serpent is still peering out of the unutterably green foliage. It shows the love act taking place in Paradise itself, then, and not after the expulsion. That's the real Fall of Man! Here for the first time humanity rejoices in the blessed tidings: they loved one another!"

the curve formed by the woman's thighs. In his opinion, the painting commingles the highest virtues of different artistic traditions — German and Italian. "Hier zeigt sich ein deutscher Meister als Erotiker von südlichster, aller-südlichster Emphatik!"[22]

The most striking thing about this painting, apart from Kaiser's devoting so much attention to it, is its ambivalence. On the one hand it appears to offer a counter-ideal to the historical anarchic situation and a reminder of what constitutes ideal creativity. The central problem of anarchy, of course, was chaos or dissociation, or in its acutest form, war — dissociation of the individual from his fellow men, of separate faculties within man, of the irrational from the rational, of nature from experience, of human nature from the institutions of society. And the longed-for solution was integration or reconciliation of these separated spheres, bringing together the things that the Fall had set asunder, restoring the mythic state of oneness which would embrace but also transcend everything that men had learned or experienced since eating of the forbidden tree. To be creative was to be motivated by this ideal, seeking for a way to use unlike or contradictory elements in interactive or productive relationships. Thus the ideal erotic goal was a complementary mating of male and female for procreative purposes; the ideal social goal, a merger of individual and group into a community; the ideal artistic goal a fusion of form and raw material, of the tangibly and intangibly real, and so on. Creativity depends on the judicious exercise of power, balancing or proportioning the heterogeneous elements in each dimension according to the ideal goal of each; hence the vision of Paradise, without which any activity will fail to realize its essential purpose.

22. "Here a German master proves himself an eroticist of southernmost, extreme southernmost power."

At the same time, however, the painting offers an interpretation of the "real Fall of Man," which, according to the art historian (obviously speaking for the playwright), consists in the attempt to juxtapose incompatibles: an act inappropriate to the place, Adam and Eve enjoying the fruits of knowledge at the very scene of their disobedience, the union of the first human couple taking place at the moment of their separation from God, the actual state of man superimposed upon the setting of his ideal original condition. It is a graphic way of picturing man's blasphemously acting as if there were no difference between creativity and sin. Is this not also a symbolic way of depicting Kassierer's, or Kaiser's, own guilt? He, too, has had an opportunity to grasp the vision but has failed to perceive its significance. Instead of the ideal, he sees the immediately or tangibly real; instead of the symbol the concrete thing; instead of thinking through his possibility to the end he accepts its apparent promise, reducing it to a personal level and then misusing it to gratify his own interests. As a consequence, the ideal is corrupted and the longing for it frustrated. Kassierer has been selfishly motivated; he has mistaken the chance to find his identity as a creator. Instead of serving the ideal, he usurps power for ends that might enhance his self-esteem.

The point is made over and over again in the play. Note, for example, Kassierer's attempts to make contact with others, either erotically or socially. Here again the circle of error begins with his ·mistake about the lady, since his hasty acceptance of a baser possibility causes him to overlook her unselfish purpose and to miss the opportunity to perform a useful service himself. Erotically, then, his desire focusses on lust and sex, and when he does glimpse the painting, all he sees are its "flesh tones," mistaking Eve for a portrait of the lady, whom he recognizes, he says wryly, "by the wrist of her hand." Kassierer's

preoccupation with sex throughout the various stages of
his search is made obvious through the play's imagery. He
leaves home after his wife fumblingly fails to light his
pipe due to its "accumulation of unused tobacco"; he
squanders money at the sports arena in order to feed the
great "conflagration" of passion he has ignited; and at
the palace of pleasure he pours "fluid powder" down the
throats of the *filles de joie* in order to "charge up their bat-
teries" and "prepare them for discharge." Nothing here
about the mysteries of Eros or the creative purpose of
human relationships; nothing but the hunt for sexual outlet or the desperate need to prove one's own potency. To
the very end, Kassierer persists in believing that a man
and a woman, solely by virtue of their physical together-
ness, constitute a value in themselves. Nevertheless, his
failures and frustrations, precisely because they destroy
that illusion, do make him gradually aware of a greater
goal. Thus when left alone with the Salvation Army lass in
the Mission after tossing his money to the crowd, he recalls the painting and makes an effort to reinterpret his
own situation in its light. "Mädchen und Mann. Uralte
Gärten aufgeschlossen [. . .] Stimme aus Baumwipfel-
stille [. . .] Mädchen und Mann — ewige Beständigkeit.
Mädchen und Mann — Fülle im Leeren. Mädchen und
Mann — vollendeter Anfang. Mädchen und Mann —
Keim und Krone. Mädchen und Mann — Sinn and Ziel
und Zweck."[23] Something of the ideal is indeed present in
this ecstasy of alliteration, yet in proclaiming an abstract
realm of paradox void of anything but himself and the girl
standing beside him, Kassierer still deludes himself, for
Paradise cannot be embodied or limited to any concrete

23. "A man and a girl. Primeval gardens opened [. . .] Voice from the
stillness of treetops [. . .] A man and a girl — eternal constancy. A man
and a girl — fullness in emptiness. A man and a girl — perfected beginning.
A man and a girl — bud and blossom. A man and a girl — meaning and
goal and purpose."

instance; the kingdom is not of this world. When the girl
betrays him he knows at last that this apparent union of
opposites is really only a sameness in difference. "Einsamkeit ist Raum. Raum ist Einsamkeit. Kälte ist Sonne.
Sonne ist Kälte. Fiebernd blutet der Leib. Fiebernd friert
der Leib." [24] Thus, all his efforts to realize oneness
through his own power turn out to be solipsistic. He tries to
be both center and circumference, and the result is that his
course leads him around in circles — and always outside
the Garden.

Kassierer's mistake with respect to the lady also has a
social implication. The differences between them are for-
midable: she is a foreigner and neither of his class nor
way of life. Yet he insists on making her the partner of his
experiences and assumes that a suitable price will be sufficient to equalize their differences and place both of them,
together, above society's laws and distinctions. The message of the painting — that creation has been passed on to
man and woman as the task of founding a new human
community based on the knowledge gained from the
Fall — is completely lost on him. Hence his use of power to
force social cohesion, not so much for the sake of wholeness as such, as for the pleasure in knowing that he himself has destroyed the barriers between people and
welded them together in an elemental ball of passion. In
the sports arena, that aim shows up blatantly in Kassierer's jubilant cry at a moment of high excitement:
"Oben und mitten und unten vermischt. Ein Heulen aus
allen Ringen — unterschiedlos. [. . .] Wogender Mensch-
heitsstrom. Entkettet — frei. Vorhänge hoch — Vor-
wände nieder. Menschheit. Freie Menschheit. Hoch und
tief — Mensch. Keine Ringe — keine Schichten — keine

24. "Solitude is peace. Space is solitude. Cold is sun. Sun is cold. The
body bleeds in fever. The body freezes in fever."

Klassen."[25] Clearly, Kassierer thinks of the antianarchic
ideal as realizable within chaos itself, for he conceives of
freedom as the absence of restraint, brotherhood as the result of eliminating all differences between human beings,
man's essential nature as that which remains when one is
stripped of pretenses and illusions, and the human spirit
as a single "howl" of passion. But this is not wholeness or a
creative union of opposites; it is the reversal of one aspect
of anarchy into its complement, a further illustration of
Kassierer's exchanging the limitations of the bank world
for a supplemental set of circumstances.

The central idea of mis-taking is developed further in
Von morgens bis mitternachts through Kaiser's ingenious
use of the semantic pun — playing with the conventional
definitions of a word in such a way that its significance or
meaning changes in the course of the action. Puns of this
sort recur throughout the play, as in Kaiser's exploitation
of the ambiguities in a word like *Wert* ("value"); but in a
few instances, notably the terms Kassierer himself uses to
describe his search, the punning is evaluative as well and
tells us much about the play's underlying pattern of intentions. I am thinking particularly of the words *Leistung,
Nacktheit, Schwindel,* and *Leidenschaft* through which
Kaiser discloses the strategy behind his protagonist's actions. The meaning of each of these terms undergoes a
doubly ironic inversion in the course of the play, for what
initially appears negative, as Kassierer interprets it, later
turns out to be positive, as effective strategy for reaching
the goal, when the words are taken in the sense appropriate to him.

The semantic range of these words is broad: *Leistung*

25. "All mixed together: above, in the middle, below. One howl from
all sides — no differences [. . .] Undulating stream of humanity. Un-
chained — free. Curtains up — pretenses down. Humanity. Free humanity.
High and low — Man. No circles — no levels — no classes."

refers among other things to "feat, effect, artistic performance" or even "solvency"; *Nacktheit* is equivalent to "nakedness, bareness, bereftness"; *Schwindel* embraces both
"giddy dizziness" and "swindle, fraud"; while *Leidenschaft* means "emotion, passion" and "suffering". *Leistung*
is the primary word, since Kassierer's aim in each sphere
of mundane experience is to bring off another "fabulous
performance" like his successful theft of the bank's money.
To justify this act — or shall we say bluntly, to prove his
potency? — he tries to create a maximal effect on those he
encounters and to push them to a point they would never
have reached on their own initiative: "Ich subventioniere
nur Höchstleistungen." [26] And the *Leistung* in each instance is bound up in his mind not only with *Nacktheit*
(removing the camouflages or barriers which prevent people from making such efforts), but also with *Schwindel*
and *Leidenschaft* (inducing a state of excitement that will
wipe out individuality and self-control in a universal community of passion). The various facets of his aim emerge
gradually in the sports arena along with his mounting en-
thusiasm after each race. "[. . .] Leiber in Bewegung.
[. . .] Ganz oben fallen die letzten Hüllen. [. . .]
Brüllende Nacktheit. Die Galerie der Leidenschaft! [. . .]
Die Beherrschung ist zum Teufel. [. . .] Das ist letzte
Ballung des Tatsächlichen. Hier schwingt es sich zu seiner
schwindelhaften Leistung auf. [. . .] Verkleidungen von
Nacktheit gestreift: Leidenschaft!" [27]

The strategy based on Kassierer's original understanding of these words is condemned by simple frustration and
ironic inversion of the intended effect. The *Leistung* he

26. "I only underwrite the best performances."
27. "[. . .] Bodies in motion [. . .] High above in the galleries the
last inhibitions fall. [. . .] A naked roar. The gallery of passion! [. . .]
Restraint gone to hell. [. . .] That's the ultimate concentration of effect.
Here it reaches a breathtaking climax. [. . .] Nakedness showing through
disguises: passion!"

aims at is a spectacular feat that would prove his power to manipulate people and events for the sake of desired values; yet the result in every case is the opposite of what he expects. The frenzied crowd at the sports arena lapses into respectful silence in the presence of a royal prince; the *fille de joie* whom he plies with champagne becomes incapable of giving him pleasure; the penitents in the Salvation Army Mission scramble for his discarded money instead of trampling it under their feet. Erotically, no less than socially, Kassierer accomplishes nothing, and in overlooking the goals suggested in the painting he only exacerbates the prevailing state of anarchy. After each of his visits to the various spheres of mundane experience he leaves a scene of disorder, broken relationships, and destruction: his mother dead at home and his wife in trauma; a racer thrown from the track and a woman crushed by the crowd; a waiter in despair and driven to suicide at the palace of pleasure; a "chaotically struggling mass" at the Mission. Kassierer himself is completely indifferent; "Es geht nicht ohne Tote ab," he says cynically, "wo andere fiebernd leben." [28] Ultimately, however, the sole *Leistung* of this would-be manipulator of experience is to annihilate his own existence. Kassierer's suicide with the revolver is ironic proof that his hope of achieving any desired end rests on turning the instrument of power against himself.

The puns on *Nacktheit* result in a similar semantic inversion. For Kassierer, taking his cue from the lady's ungloved hand in his and then from her "portrait" in the painting, the original root meaning of the word is physical: "Hart auf den Leib rücken — und das Mäntelchen vom Leib, dann zeigt sich was!" [29] Values, in other words,

28. "Some are bound to die when others live feverishly."
29. "Close in on the body and off with its cloak; then you'll see something!"

come from stripping — from tearing off masks and costumes in order to uncover the beauty beneath, from removing inhibitions and restraints in order to release the genuine emotion within. Yet in acting on this assumption Kassierer only discovers that human nature, naked, is not what he had expected it to be: the spontaneity of the sports crowd is exposed as a conditioned reflex; the glitter and mystery of the soubrettes is unmasked as ugliness; the contrition and confession of the Salvation Army witnesses turn out to be sheer hypocrisy. Ultimately, then, and again ironically, the only thing Kassierer has been able to strip away are his own illusions. The *Nacktheit* he discovers is the truth about himself and the world, both governed by self-interest and power. Beneath fleshly appearances there is the skeleton of death.

The strategy suggested by the word *Schwindel* also turns out to be an ironical inversion of what Kassierer originally intends it to be. He aims at effects that will put the various types of people he meets in a paroxysm of giddy excitement so that they will yield their maximum value to him (*Schwindel* as dizziness); and he believes this can best be accomplished by pretending to be one of their own kind and beating them at their own game (*Schwindel* as deceit). Thus, in the palace of pleasure he aims to bowl them over in the assumed role of playboy, disguised in tuxedo, cape, and shawl, brandishing a bamboo cane with a gold knob. "Auf in den Kampf, Torero —— Was einem nicht alles auf die Lippen kommt. Man ist ja geladen. Alles — einfach alles. Torero — Carmen. Caruso. Den Schwindel irgendwo mal gelesen — haftengeblieben."[30] Yet Kassierer fools no one through his *Schwindel*,

30. "Into the fray, Torero —— It's amazing what all you can find to say! I'm positively loaded. Everything — simply everything. Torero — Carmen. Caruso. Read all that malarkey sometime somewhere — and it stuck in my mind."

and the only one bewildered by the shenanigans is himself. He can't even handle the jargon of this mundane sphere, misreading the French menu, mishearing "drei" for "dry," mistaking the name of a cognac for champagne. All this posturing, then, is actually imposturing; he is a fraud and a fake. Instead of fooling others he has only deceived himself; instead of finding his identity through playing a series of roles — just as much a "theft" as his stealing the money — he has only frustrated his chances of really belonging. And this effort to exercise power by putting others off guard winds up by throwing Kassierer himself totally off balance. The ultimate *Schwindel* for him is the ill-considered search itself, seemingly a direct line to somewhere but actually a circular course leading nowhere, a futile cycle of errors cutting through the vacuum outside him and the void within.

So inverting his protagonist's intentions, Kaiser passes judgment on his own (real or imagined) sin in trying to exercise power that is not proper to him in a world that is not his to control. For the playwright, however, as distinct from his protagonist, this point of no return also represents a point of new departure. In the end lies his beginning, "end" not only in the sense of termination, therefore, but also in the sense of goal or of what shall determine purpose in the future. Having exposed the original sense of his protagonist's strategy as negative, Kaiser turns the tables once more by indicating how their very negativism becomes the way toward fulfillment of his quest. Hence the *Leistung*, which negates the self as the center of existence, opens the way to awareness of a worthier goal; the *Nacktheit*, remaining after all appearances and illusions have been burned off, becomes a solid frame of truth and knowledge; the *Schwindel* acts like a centrifugal force in extracting essences from accidentals. Thus Kaiser doubles his punning into paradox.

All this play on mistaken meanings comes to a climax with a pun on *Leidenschaft* which leads directly to the strategy Kaiser has in mind. Here again, the sense of the term, as of the other key expressions just discussed, is initially determined by Kassierer's reaction to his routine existence in the bank world. For him, *Leidenschaft* originally means unrestrained emotion, overwhelming passion, the tides of sensation. And in dealing with this quality, he is again both curiously detached and full of self-interest. He wants to manipulate the course of his experience without regard to its eventual consequences, to remain aloof and derive his pleasure from making others dance to his tune. The *effect* is all-important, for it is to prove his power to affect a situation without being swept away himself. Once more, however, an ironic inversion of intentions indicates that this sense of *Leidenschaft* is not proper to the playwright, that it is in fact only a further strategic mistake with respect to his goal. Kassierer's attempts to raise emotions higher and higher, by offering a corresponding price for results, collapse when the people involved sink into senselessness trying to keep up with his bidding; and his hope of burning away all differences between individuals, melting them into a single ball of passion, backfires when the emotions he has aroused carry them in opposite directions or set them in wild competition against each other. The height of irony is reached in the Salvation Army Mission when Kassierer tosses his remaining marks to the assembled penitents only to see them "ignited" by this unexpected windfall into doing "heated battle for the money." After turning the place upside down, they "tumble over each other to the door and roll outside" — not a unifying ball of passion after all, just a chaotic conglomerate of self-interests.

Kaiser turns this negative judgment of *Leidenschaft* into a positive strategy by reviving the word's correlative

meaning of "suffering," "endurance," or "pain." By the end
of the play the term no longer refers to the pathos of sen-
sations, but to the pathos of suffering; not to the manipulation of emotions in order to demonstrate potency, but to
the endurance of apparent impotence; not to passion at all
in the mundane sense, but to the Passion. This shift in
meaning becomes unmistakable when Kassierer recalls
the steps of his search as Stations of the Cross and then
stages his death as a pseudocrucifixion, arms stretched
out in silhouette against the Cross.

Once more the question arises: What is one to make of
this somewhat belated allusion to the Christian myth? It
would be unwarranted, I think, to assume that Kassierer
at this point becomes a secular variant of Christ or that his
suicide stands for the act by which Kaiser frees himself for
a traditional *imitatio Christi*. For this, the parallels are too
fragmentary and the evidence too thin. Furthermore, the
Passion is only one aspect of the mythical background in
Von morgens bis mitternachts; the other deals with the
prelude to that event, the story of man's Fall, which was
introduced much earlier into the play through the Cranach painting. Kaiser was probably attracted to the Christian myth, then, not because it was Christian but because
it was part of a total nonhistorical pattern of action illus-
trating the strategy he had in mind. The myth undoubtedly enhanced the significance of his quest by surround-
ing it with a religious aura. More to the point, it offered an
ideal order of values to set in dialectical counterpoint to
the actual, or personal, problem Kaiser was trying to cope
with in the play. As we know, the great need of that time
was for an integrative principle to offset the divisive
forces of anarchy. Kaiser's substitute for this absolute was
the total Christian myth — secularized, stripped of all
doctrinal implications, and transferred onto the level of
dialectic. It proved insufficient to encompass the general

historical situation, but it provided a justification for his own activity and enabled him to reevaluate the circle of routine existence as a cycle of meaningful change.

Above all, the Christian myth was for Kaiser an apposite illustration of the universal pattern of death and rebirth. Transformation in the spirit is implicit in Christ's martyrdom, and this promise is spelled out fully by Paul in his epistles to the Christian congregations: "For as in Adam all die, even so in Christ shall all be made alive" (I Cor. 15:22); "Therefore if any man be in Christ, he is a new creature; old things are passed away; behold, all things are become as new" (II Cor. 5:17). This version of the rebirth pattern exercised a special strategic appeal, moreover, in that it embodied the paradox by which defeat is turned into victory through the mysterious alchemy of sacrifice: "He that loseth his life for my sake shall find it." Like many anarchic poets, who desperately needed such reassurance, Kaiser also regarded the Passion as an archetypal demonstration that human degradation could be raised to triumph and individual isolation overcome in a universal brotherhood of spirit. Also like them, he seized upon the strategic essence of the Christian myth, seeing in it another version of the "fortunate fall," that remarkable expression occuring in diverse cultures of the belief that man's greatest glory becomes possible only at the moment of his deepest despair. Thus Adam's sin brought evil into the world and yet prepared for mankind's redemption through the "second Adam," the crucified Christ of the Cross; similarly, the hero in tragedy demolishes the world in his vain attempt to eradicate injustice, yet by his death enables life and restores our faith in fundamental order. In the myth of *felix culpa*, the hero paradoxically dies that he may live, falls that he may rise, suffers that he may learn, enacting that transformation from innocence to experience to knowledge which is the essence of any rebirth.[31] In the Passion, then, such purposeful suffering reaches its apotheosis, for here the crucified becomes identical with the savior.

Kaiser, of course, extracted from this mystery only what he needed to encompass his situation. The problem begins with Kassierer's sudden awareness of being fundamentally alienated from the rationalized and functional world of anarchic society. Ironically, he "counts" for nothing in a position which requires him to do nothing but "count." When he steals the bank's money, then, Kassierer is motivated by the desire to reverse this situation, to use this means to acquire goods he has never owned, and to establish purpose in an otherwise meaningless existence. This attempt is fundamentally ambivalent. On the one hand, it is genuinely creative, for he aims at making a new man of himself, at remaking life according to his newly found sense of value; on the other hand, it is clearly sinful in that it involves the use of illegitimate power with the frank intent of forcing the world to answer his needs. Symbolized initially as a crime, indicating violation of the law which should govern his place in society and his relationship to other men, this offense emerges in the course of the play as a sin as well because it involves transgression against the ultimate orders of reality and the laws of his own existence. Kassierer's attempt to bring about change through exchanging one set of circumstances for another is one aspect of that sin; so is his attempt to make communication with others possible by posing as one of them, by pretending to speak their language. I have called this sin a mis-take, despite the innocuous sound of the word, because the term embraces *misappropriation* (the

31. See Herbert Weisinger, *Tragedy and the Paradox of the Fortunate Fall* (in particular, p. 271), to which I am indebted for this discussion.

theft and fraudulent use of power) and *misunderstanding* (the failure to perceive the true meaning of a situation and to act accordingly), both of which are implicit in the original offense. No doubt there are biographical counterparts to this offense, any one of which might be subsumed under the general category of demonstrating potency, but the most pertinent for our purposes concerns Kaiser's own occupation as artist. From this point of view the mis-take refers to an error about the nature of human creativity or about the limits of his own role as creator. This seems to be the import of the Cranach painting, which, as we saw, interprets the true Fall as man's attempt to rejoin the incompatibles that were introduced into existence through his own disobedience. In the painting, as in the life of Kassierer-Kaiser, who takes his cue from it, sin and creativity are blasphemously juxtaposed in the assumption that Paradise can be regained with the power stolen from God and that man can reproduce in actuality, or by his own efforts, the ideal possibility represented by his original condition before the Fall. The mis-take foretold in the painting, and subsequently acted out in Kassierer's abortive search, consists then in carrying on as if there were no difference between creativity and sin, as if the vision were realizable in actuality, as if, so to speak, man might continue to eat of the forbidden tree and yet enjoy his fulfillment in Paradise. It was, in short, a mis-take about the meaning of what is meant to be.

Now just as sin accompanies creativity, and the awareness of a mistake arises through trying to act upon its assumptions, so the right meaning for Kaiser emerges from exhausting the possibilities of error. His true identity discloses itself through failure in playing a series of false roles. Experience, in other words, is Kaiser's purgatory; the same flames that had burned as desire — and the play is full of images of fire — turn out to be the flames of purgation, purifying while they punish, revealing what might become even as they cleanse away what must not be.

Kaiser undergoes a mode of purification determined by the nature of his offense. It is that special kind of suffering known as disillusionment, in which pride in setting one's course is shattered by failure and by the increasing certainty of having made an initial false step. What destroys — and then cures — him is an intellectual agony, the necessity of rethinking the grounds of his actions and of reviewing his dialectic in order to establish the proper relationship between actual and ideal, between the reality of everyday existence and the reality of man's essential nature. Kassierer's futile search for value seems now in retrospect to be a genuine *Leidensweg* — involuntary, to be sure, and originally without awareness of its significance — a projection of the playwright's own painful course toward identity and the only way for him to fulfill this quest.

(Is it not possible that Kaiser's famous formula for writing drama might have developed from the psychological necessity to repeat this process ritualistically in work after work? Guilty of acting upon impulse without considering the consequences, and of translating impersonal goals into personal motives, he imposed the rigorous discipline of "thinking a thought through to the end" as punishment — or preventative — for succumbing to this peculiar temptation to sin.)

Kaiser's purgatorial *Leidensweg* is redemptive as well as punitive. It is his way to salvation because the disillusionment he experiences makes it possible for him to discover, and accept, the truth about his place in the scheme of things. In this sense the *Stationen* are actually stages of perception; they mark the moments when Kassierer-Kaiser comes paradoxically ever closer to the goal as each successive phase of his search turns out to be false. Kassie-

rer himself believes he has reached that goal in the Salvation Army Mission when he tosses the remnants of his
misbegotten power to the assembled penitents: "Von
Schlacken befreit lobt sich meine Seele hoch hinauf —
ausgeschmolzen aus diesen glühenden zwei Tiegeln: Be-
kenntnis und Buße."[32] He is wrong, however, because
confession and penitence are not enough to wipe out the
pride still lingering in his words; the purgatorial process is
not yet finished. Just as the skeletal image had predicted
on the open field of snow, the ultimate result of his search
would be *Abgebranntheit*, a complete loss of everything
through fire, power consumed by power. Only when the
self has burned utterly away can its essence be extracted;
the suffering imposed on him without his volition must
terminate in a deliberate act of sacrifice. By having Kassierer commit suicide before the Cross, that traditional
place for the transvaluation of values, Kaiser indicates
that he himself had passed judgment on the Old Man in
order to make possible the promise of the New and that
he had found a new "principle of purpose"[33] in exchanging the first Adam for the second. His model henceforth
would no longer be the presumptuous creator trying to
imitate God, but the suffering servant and son of Man; not
Adam whose sin had estranged man from his essential nature, but Christ who had come to remind the world of the
pattern from which it had strayed.[34] He had, I believe,
found his longed-for identity at last in the martyr's role.

32. "Free of dross my soul is extolled on high — purified in the glowing
crucibles of confession and penitence."

33. Burke, *A Grammar of Motives*, p. 311.

34. For an interpretation of Christian doctrine similar to the one on
which this analogy is based, see Reinhold Niebuhr, *Beyond Tragedy*. The
distinction between sin and creativity, and the notion of an ideal possibility, both derive from this book. For the former, see chapter 11, "The
Things That Are and the Things That Are Not"; for the latter, chapter 14,
"The Kingdom Is Not of This World."

Von morgens bis mitternachts ends at this point without any further indication of what Kaiser understood by this role or how it might be worked out pragmatically in his own life. This is fair enough, of course, and any attempt to speculate upon the implications of this strategy can only be justified by the conviction that these are already contained in the play and that Kaiser himself invites us to explore them. To "think a thought through to the end," enacting an intellectual process on stage, so to speak, is to call for public participation in the undertaking, is in effect to broaden the strategy so that the taking of meanings becomes a partaking and his private problem a matter of communal concern. Kaiser does not insist, as for example Brecht was shortly to do, that an audience draw its own conclusions from what he shows them, but he does ask for a greater intellectual concentration than was previously required in the German theater, in the hope of sparking an exchange between playwright and playgoer, at least in the realm of ideas. Picking up Kaiser's cues, then, let us venture some conclusions about the strategy implicit in his gravitation to the martyred Christ of the Cross.

Martyrdom, we noted, embodies the paradox by which a negative condition of suffering becomes a positive way of doing; the martyr's passional is his act. (Hence, as Burke points out, the interchangeability of these terms in most accounts of martyrdom.)[35] This seeming contradiction is resolved in the notion of sacrifice, that is, in the voluntary submission to suffering — death, or mere victimization, it makes no difference — for the sake of something else. Implicit in any martyrdom is the idea of mediation; the martyr elects to deny himself in order to serve. Inasmuch as his act is a vicarious one, furthermore, in which he substitutes his own suffering in place of someone else's,

35. *A Grammar of Motives*, p. 271.

the martyr becomes a scapegoat for others, ritualistically atoning for the iniquities they both share. Thus Christ, the prototype, offers himself as intermediary between the human and the divine, willingly taking on the burden of man's sin in order to effect his redemption; and the Christian martyr emulates that matchless act by renouncing his own life in willing service to this ideal. The act embodied in his passion involves a transformation of values, not merely for himself, but also for those whose own attitudes are changed from witnessing his exemplary deed. And, of course, although this must not enter into his motivation, the martyr knows that his *Verdienst* will be proportional to his *Dienst*, that he deserves according to the way he serves, that he saves himself in filling another's need.

We have already encountered the notion of the scapegoat in Kaiser's slaying his protagonist for the sake of his own rebirth. It now seems likely that the playwright's own relationship to his audience is much like Kassierer's relationship to him, for the first qualification of a scapegoat is that he should share the sin of those for whom he becomes the "chosen vessel of iniquity," [36] and in the person of his protagonist Kaiser does clearly align himself with modern capitalist society in its cardinal offense. Like everyone else in the world of mundane experience, Kaiser-Kassierer overestimates the "existential buying power of money," letting his ends be determined by this means, treating it as a commodity with a value in its own right, acting as if it were exchangeable on a quid pro quo basis for equivalent values of a different kind. This sin is defined in socio-economic terms — underlying the critique of capitalism which most critics assume to be the main import of the play — but the money image encourages us to believe that Kaiser is referring to the misuse of power in general, whatever

36. Ibid., p. 301. See also pp. 406f.

the sphere of application, whenever it is used primarily for self-gratification or the fulfillment of personal desires. This, at any rate, is the sin Kaiser-Kassierer discovers in all those he meets during the course of his abortive search, and by the end of the play he confesses that he too belongs among these fellow-sinners and is ready now to join this "guild of the guilty." Thus the negative fact of guilt becomes his positive means of identification, and in representing society's sin through his own sin, then offering himself in its place by way of atonement, Kaiser does in fact become society's scapegoat. This sacrificial act settles the original problem of his alienation, for it makes him part of society, yet at the same time raises him above the group through his willingness to confess and suffer for what they have both been guilty of.

A further dimension to this sin seems peculiar to Kaiser's own position as a writer. We noted that when Kassierer shifts from the routine world of the bank to the chaotic world of mundane experience, it is to bring about change in his own life through supplanting one set of circumstances with another. This effort is intended to secure him values he has been deprived of and to compensate him for the sense of not counting in his work. The power he steals is meant to prove his potency, and clearly he feels that his best chances for this are in spheres of activity outside his own profession. The power-image, we suggested, might refer to the problem of creativity in various spheres; we are now ready to guess that it also has to do with Kaiser's fear of overstepping his function as dramatist and of violating language's mediate position between life and art. Behind the socio-economic message of *Von morgens bis mitternachts*, which is undoubtedly present, the playwright is taking himself to task for the way in which he has handled, or was tempted to handle, his own medium.

Kaiser was on good grounds in equating language with money; after all, language is also a medium of exchange and a means for obtaining desired consequences; like money, again, it is an instrument for assessing values whose worth depends on whether one's linguistic resources have been properly or improperly employed. This analogy has been very carefully worked out. Like his protagonist's mistake with respect to money, Kaiser's mistake with respect to language consists in a misunderstanding about its real nature and in misappropriating it solely for his own use. He "steals" a certain number of words from among the large sums in current circulation and treats them as his own property, assigning them an arbitrary meaning restricted solely to their customary market value and utilizing them to achieve immediate effects without concern for their eventual consequences. Words are looked upon as commodities, to be exchanged on a quid pro quo basis for other goods, their buying power in direct ratio to the amount he is prepared to expend. And as objects for bargaining — witness Kassierer's use of the key terms *Nacktheit, Schwindel,* and *Leidenschaft* — Kaiser manipulates words with literal-minded consistency and with singular disregard for their inherent ambiguity or their symbolic potential. He has, in brief, overlooked the fact that language is a *symbolic medium of exchange*: symbolic because its value resides not in any physical qualities of the things constituting it, but in its ability to substitute, or stand for relationships between a thing and its potential consequences; a medium of exchange in the sense that its purpose is the making of meanings. Through verbal interaction it is possible to arrive at some agreement about the relationships between the thing signified and the thing signifying. To use language effectively as an instrument for intellectual meaning, where a "thing is more significantly what it makes possible than what it im-

mediately is," one must subordinate "things in their
immediacy . . . to what they portend and give evidence
of," and by means of discourse reach accord on what shall
make sense for those who use the words as their means of
communication.[37] That Kaiser-Kassierer does not even ap-
proximate this function is proved by his failure to find the
kind of value he seeks: the taking of meanings never becomes a partaking for him and what he intends is invariably inverted into what was intended to be.

The basic mistake, and its inevitable results, are prefig-
ured symbolically in the scene where Kassierer visits the
lady in her hotel room. This scene masterfully reveals the
multiplicity of mistaken meanings that arise from various
responses to the Cranach painting. For the lady, the Cranach is a "naive" work of art which gives her an opportunity to sacrifice her own comfort and resources in order to
further her son's career; for Kassierer, who overlooks its
symbolic implications, the painting is quite literally a portrait that confirms the possibility of attaining his desires.
These different points of view, the taking and mis-taking
of the object's meaning, result in an exchange that is neither conversation nor communication but a talking past
one another in the vain attempt to try to make sense out
of what the other has in mind. Here anarchy has determined the very process of thought. The scene dramatizes
what we later perceive, namely, that Kaiser-Kassierer mis-
uses power in trying to force the union of irreconcilables;
that he moves out of his depth in assuming a fraudulent
role in a sphere to which he does not belong; and that the
capricious use of his medium is a transgression against its
and his own nature as well as against society. For Kaiser is
really Kassierer after all, the man in charge of a most important medium of human exchange, and he has violated

37. John Dewey, *Experience and Nature*, p. 128, defining cognitive
meaning, or intellectual significance.

this trust through mistaking the nature of his means and his proper function with respect to it. He has, to put it another way, sinned against the creative possibilities of the medium itself.

Once again the corrective strategy is supplied by the martyr image. A cashier, like a martyr, is a man who serves: he identifies with his function, merges with his office, and hides behind his work. He finds his justification in an instrumentality, and agency becomes his purpose. So the poet, dealing in symbols, performs a mediatory role — expediting the transactions between life and art, between actuality and vision, between existence and essence, between the condition in which men find themselves and the condition to which they might aspire. He reminds men that value does not exist in the thing possessed but in what it represents, and assists them to arrive at agreement about the relationships between the thing signified and the thing signifying. The linguistic "cashier" is, then, a midwife of meanings with the function of making men aware of what had hitherto been unperceived and of opening up new possibilities for human attitudes and actions.

Most of the problems implicit in Kaiser-Kassierer's situation are disposed of through this strategic adoption of the martyr's role — among others, his feeling of not "counting" in a position that requires him to do nothing but count. When he is awakened into consciousness by the lady's unexpected appearance, Kassierer suddenly sees his occupation as a mere routine operation for the rationalized ends of a system that will not recognize him as an individual or reward him with a share in its profits. His job appears as a perfunctory operation, assisting others to deal in goods he has no hope of attaining himself, and he performs it impersonally as part of an impersonal machine. Although the symbols of power must flow through his hands in their movement from owner to owner, he has no control over the exchange and no sense of fulfilling a purpose in any way pertinent to himself. He is being used without feeling useful. Thus Kaiser-Kassierer goes about his work — or, as we might say after analyzing the play, exercises his art — without perceiving any value or justification in what he was or what he was doing. The martyr image allowed Kaiser to take the function itself as his purpose and the perfunctory task of the "cashier" as an essential operation in the economy of men's affairs. His was the responsibility for handling the means by which men assess their values and arrive at meanings. His use lay in his usefulness to others, therefore, and the value of his work in being an instrumentality of human exchange. Service became his substitute for power, and through it he found a way of identifying his private concerns with the public good.

A second problem implicit in Kaiser's situation, and in a sense the obverse of the first, is the need to experience change — to escape the self-perpetuating circle in which one event seems the same as another and each determines its successor as it had been determined by the one preceding it. In the too-ordered world of the bank, and subsequently in the chaotic world of mundane experience under an entirely different set of circumstances, Kaiser-Kassierer discovers an essentially static, predictive condition in which meaning has been replaced by mere operation, and purposeful behavior by habit and conditioned reflex. Because events in anarchy do not lead to consequences, they are of no consequence themselves; because there is no interaction among the disparate things of this world there is no consciousness of their being involved in change. The martyr image, however, indicated that fundamental change does not originate in events or in the simple alteration of circumstances, but that it begins within, as a transformation in thought or spirit. *Wandlung* is the term most frequently used by Kaiser's expressionist contemporaries for this inner regeneration, and like him they derived their inspiration from the Passion of Christ. But in his case, the religious connotations are deliberately secularized, for the *Wandlung* he has in mind is basically intellectual; it is primarily a mental process, a change in one's way of thinking about a thing, in the meaning it has for one, in one's state of mind. Although such a conversion may seem to occur with the Paulinian force of a sudden insight, as indeed it does for Kassierer when he impulsively throws himself against the Cross, it actually takes place only after prolonged struggle with one's thoughts, after an intellectual agony of grappling with meanings modified and remodified in the process of trying to act upon them. Perhaps the most significant difference between *Von morgens bis mitternachts* and Kaiser's more finished expressionistic dramas is that the struggle here is still experiential, bearing the traces of his own trial-and-error search for *his* meaning of *Wandlung*, whereas the later plays project the struggle in "purer" form as a more dispassionate intellectual exercise, a true *Denkspiel*, in which we too are invited to participate. The original necessity of punishing himself for not thinking a thought through to the end turns finally into a public ritual.

Transformation begins, in Kaiser's book, with the consciousness of possibilities never known previously. Not until the lady appears to Kassierer and touches him with desire is he moved toward change, or even made aware of its existence. In fact, the very meaning of the word arises for him only from the contrast between what is (or has been) and what might be. Thus an idea — or ideal or Vision, to use Kaiser's own expression — is a precondition of *Wandlung* as he understands it, necessary to set the process in motion and also to provide the actual state of affairs with its dialectical counterpart. Just as history would be

"a meaningless succession of events" without some notion
of purpose, so would there be no reason for undertaking
anything at all without the "perception of what might be
but is not, the promise of things hoped for, the symbol of
things not seen"; ideas are "the obverse of action." [38]
Between the idea and the action, however, lies a road of
error whose end result is truth. Kaiser-Kassierer begins his
Wandlung with a mistake about the lady, follows it with
another about the Cranach painting, and goes on to suffer
a series of disillusionments which only the termination of
his long search discloses as stages of perception. If Adam
is the necessary prelude to Christ in the myth of mankind's redemption, then "sinning," the attempt to bring
about change through one's own efforts, is also the basis of
human creativity. For in the drama of human life, new
conditions arise because one has attempted to realize an
ideal, even though its fulfillment does not rest alone on
man's power. Martyrdom remains the best hope of transformation.

A new definition of creativity is implicit in this way of
thinking: it means assisting things to attain their potential
and contributing to the renewal of life by bringing about
new changes in meaning. Language, the "natural bridge"
between existence and essence, [39] is the primary instrumentality for this purpose, and it is apparent that Kaiser,
converted to a new sense of what it means to be Kassierer,
serves his medium faithfully in the mature works following this one. He becomes a dealer in linguistic exchanges.
The basic strategy is dialectical: it tries to cope with
meaninglessness through "the possibilites of linguistic
transformation," [40] formulating and reformulating mean-

38. Ibid., p. 350.
39. Ibid., p. 167. "Yet there is a natural bridge that joins the gap between existence and essence; namely, communication, language, discourse."
40. Burke, *A Grammar of Motives*, p. 402.

ings as they interact with each other and are tested against external events. This process is clearly taking place in *Von morgens bis mitternachts*, even if it is still imperfectly worked out, so that at the end of the play things do look different from the way they looked at the beginning. "Value" has been redefined; the sense of the words Kassierer uses has changed from his initial conception of them; the role of "cashier" has another meaning for Kaiser than the one he set out with. Even the tripartite division so much favored by dialecticians (and the later Kaiser) may be discerned in the way Kaiser-Kassierer has transcended the original situation. If the scheme has not been perceived as such until now, it is because the formal structure of the play does not reflect it. Kaiser has asked us to assume the first step and left us to deduce the last one. With respect to the problem of "not counting," for example, the first step in the scheme shows Kaiser-Kassierer's awareness of being impersonally used in the rationalized world of the bank, the second his attempt to use its power personally for his own ends in the chaotic world of mundane experience, and the third his transcendence of both conditions by identifying himself with a larger impersonal purpose, thereby proving his usefulness by electing to be of use to others. A similar progression can be detected for solving the problems of change, creativity, and alienation. In each instance, the situation is transformed by dialectic, the meaning of events is remade by thinking them through. Kaiser admits in essays that accompany his later work to having derived the method from Socrates. He seems also to have taken the further Platonic step of believing that dialectic is not only the means to the good or valuable in life, but the way of the good life as well.

5

The Strategy of Reassembly
Bertolt Brecht's
Mann ist Mann

ANY CRITIC OF BRECHT will be tempted, sooner or later, to resort to Polonius's devious method of arriving at certainty: through indirections find directions out. Brecht himself has shown the way. Perhaps you know the much-repeated story of his antics while still a schoolboy at the Gymnasium in Augsburg. Young Bertolt, like one of his close friends, was not doing well in foreign languages, the friend in Latin, Brecht in French. For both boys the final examinations turned out to be a disaster: low grades, biting comments, papers cluttered with corrections in red ink. The friend erased some of the marks on his paper, substituted correct answers, and took his examination back to the teacher. Unfortunately, the ruse was detected and the feckless lad punished for his dishonesty. Brecht, on the other hand, procured his own bottle of red ink, marked some answers wrong although they were actually right, and then went to the teacher with a diffident inquiry about his errors. The embarrassed professor apologized for his oversights and hastened to compensate by giving the unlucky victim a higher grade. Brecht moved up to the next class in triumph, a happier, if not also a wiser, man.

I am sure you will understand why I, for one, should find this story a bit disarming. Doubts arise as to just how many professorial legs Brecht might have pulled in his lifetime, or continues to pull from his side of the grave; and sheer self-defense leads me to wonder whether Brecht ever, really, seriously means what he says. A professor may be forgiven for not approving publicly of young Bertolt's strategy in this situation, yet I suppose he must privately admire this adroit way of turning humiliation into advantage. No one knows whether Brecht felt that self-deprecation was always a fair tactic for coming out on top; nevertheless he came to find it increasingly attractive as the years rolled by. The "wisdom of cowardice" was his eventual name for it, a quality embodied with sure effect in such splendid scoundrels as the good-bad judge Azdak in *Der kaukasische Kreidekreis* (*The Caucasian Chalk Circle*).

Brecht is never more disarming than when commenting on his own work. About the earliest plays in particular he can be both disparaging and effusive. After a quarter of a century he looks back at *Baal*, for example, and concludes flatly, "Ich gebe zu (und warne): dem Stück fehlt Weisheit."[1] Similarly with *Mann ist Mann*, after admitting that time and audience reaction had made him uncertain about his original intentions, Brecht spends many pages speculating on what he might have been trying to do. He claims no interest in having the last word and even goes out of his way to invite counterargument, as in this aside to the reader: "Aber vielleicht gelangen Sie zu einer ganz anderen Ansicht. Wogegen ich am wenigsten etwas ein-

1. "I admit (and warn you) that the play lacks wisdom." Bertolt Brecht, "Bei Durchsicht meiner ersten Stücke" (March, 1954), *Gesammelte Werke*, 17:949.

zuwenden habe." [2] Yet he offers so many opinions, about this or any other work, that he is almost bound to hit the right nail on the head ultimately.

Some critics find this free and easygoing attitude ominous. It is whispered that Brecht was never too sure of his intentions and that this reflects a deep moral ambiguity in his own nature. He has even been chided for holding a "neutralist or indifferentist view [that] militates against the desire to affirm moral tenets." [3] More charitable voices explain that Brecht's leaning toward circumlocutions and reformulations arose from his later need, as a confirmed Marxist, to absolve the intellectual sins of his youth, a suggestion which Brecht himself seems to credit in claiming that the truth had often stood "dimly" before his eyes in the early twenties, but that he had been prevented from seeing it because of his excessive zeal and "disputatious, contradicting nature." [4] Certainly with respect to his early work Brecht becomes on occasion just another self-justifying author, straining hard to reinterpret pre-Marxist treatment in Marxist terminology. Thus he describes the figure of Baal as "asocial, but in an asocial society." Of the curious personal-metaphysical stuggle between two men in his *Im Dickicht der Städte* he writes, that at one point, without knowing it, he had been "sehr nahe an dem wirklichen Kampf, der vor sich ging and den ich nur idealisierte, am Klassenkampf." [5] Like much of what Brecht

2. "But perhaps you'll arrive at a quite different opinion. I would be the last to object to that." Bertolt Brecht, "Vorrede zu *Mann ist Mann*" (April, 1927), *Gesammelte Werke*, 17:978. Brecht was always of this opinion. Of *Leben des Galilei*, for instance, he wrote, "Der Stückschreiber wünschte nicht das letzte Wort zu haben" ("The playwright did not want to have the last word"). *Werke*, 17:1133.

3. Ronald Gray, *Bertolt Brecht*, p. 45.

4. Brecht, *Gesammelte Werke*, 17:945.

5. "Very near to the real struggle going on [around me], that is, the class struggle, which I only idealized." Ibid., p. 949.

says, these remarks are disarming not simply because they are partly true and partly false, but because he actually means what he says without being able to convince us that he always says — or knows — what he means.

From a more positive point of view, Brecht's reluctance to leave well enough alone, to let the works be their own commentary, indicates a genuine attempt to surmount the limitations time always imposes on a work's relevance. I think Brecht was supremely, even obsessively, concerned with pertinence — with the contemporary validity of a work, of course, but also with its continuing validity in the face of changing historical circumstances. Always oriented to his audiences, and finely attuned to developments in the world about him, he aimed to describe "die Handlungsweise der Menschen unserer Zeit"[6] in a way that would reveal men's fundamental behavioral patterns and also allow him to influence those patterns through his work. Although he did not make the naturalist's or documentarist's mistake of restricting himself to actual conditions, nevertheless by committing himself so wholeheartedly to historical relevance and by making history, the actual course of events, the subject of his work, Brecht necessarily lessened the chances of any play's surviving the moment that had originally called it forth. The problem is an old one, and Brecht's various efforts to solve it are well worth noting. In later works he used proverbs and parables for this purpose, thereby universalizing the particular case. More radical, and entirely modern, was his policy of making changes in a work — in subject matter, idea, or form; in the style of acting or manner of production; in his interpretations or theories — any changes whatsoever that would underscore the work's funda-

6. "Contemporary modes of action," or "ways in which people in our time go about their business." Ibid., p. 972.

mental meaning to an audience or assist in bringing out
"the truth," as he once put it, "behind the truth." For
him there was nothing sacred about the structural elements of a work; what *was* important was the principle
or law revealed by the various ways in which those elements could be arranged.

This pliability largely accounts for the perennial up-to-
dateness of Brecht's work and for the extraordinary impact it has on successive generations of playgoers. None of
the other dramatists studied in this series can match him
in this regard. Wedekind speaks to us still, sometimes,
through his choice of sex as a central metaphor, but he has
long since been outdone in exploiting its possibilities, and
the need of coming to terms with his own problems made
him lose sight too soon of the metaphor's public or meta-
sexual implications. Kaiser, for all his versatility, never advanced very far beyond his early Vision of the New Man,
expending his considerable energies in the search for ever
more private and recondite ways of varying that theme
even though it was already passé after the first World
War. And Hauptmann, who was originally acclaimed for
always waving his banner in the wind of the times, suf-
fered the unkindest fate of all, since time seemed to prove
that he had been using the fluctuations of fashion just to
propel himself ever higher up his Olympian heights. In
the end, Hauptmann almost disappeared from mortal
view, an oracle from on high whose voice was seldom
heeded even though it never uttered a false word. Significantly, all three dramatists turned to myth or their own
mythical inventions finally in the hope of universalizing a
personal situation; whereas Brecht, at a comparable stage
in his career, drew his material from history or traditional
fables already worked in literature. Like all great dramatists, as Bentley expresses it, Brecht constantly changed
the aspects of his work in order to provide "an image of

the age as a whole, picturing its principal conflicts and
triumphs (and failures . . .)."[7]

Brecht first attracted attention by nipping at the big
dogs' heels. All five of his earliest works owe much of their
character to Brecht's harassment of his older contemporaries, the expressionists, and their ideals. Like them he
wrote against the background of the anarchic situation —
a world without central or absolute value, its system of
pieties broken, human relationships reduced to the functional, the separate spheres of existence rationalized, the
irrational manifesting itself everywhere — but unlike
them he takes this situation for granted and rejects their
hope of coping with it through a transcendental strategy.
His own answers were anything but certain in these early
years; in fact, such orientation as there is derives to a
large extent from his opposition to the strategies of other
writers. In setting out to expose these as illusionary and
unrealistic, Brecht probably hoped to conceal the uncertainty of his own position by the vehemence with which
he attacked the falseness or inadequacy of someone else's.
Perhaps this is the origin of the ambiguous stance already
noted; in any event, Brecht's feinting gave him time to explore the nature of anarchy and to test out various ways of
approaching it. A brief look at his earliest plays from this
point of view has the advantage of allowing us to trace
how one type of historical strategy is beginning to give
way to another, very different way of encompassing the
same general situation.

Brecht found it necessary, first of all, to clarify the nature and function of the poet. One of the illusions most favored by anarchic writers concerned their role as prophet
or seer, the proclaimer of good tidings about a "real" life
found only in the spirit. The radical expressionist elevated

7. Eric Bentley, *The Life of the Drama*, p. 115.

himself into a high priest of *Geist* (the Spirit), that divine factor in man which enables him to penetrate the shadows of this earthly cave to the platonic absolutes beyond. The expressionist's mission was to reach the essence of things, the reality behind nature and experience, and to embody this in unchanging forms, thereby revealing the truth of things to others even though his doing so might isolate him from the rest of mankind and make him unsuitable for worldly life. Georg Kaiser calculates these possibilities brilliantly in *Der gerettete Alkibiades* (*Alcibiades Saved*), a dramatization of how Socrates suffers a mishap on the battlefield (he gets a cactus thorn in his foot and cannot move because of the pain) and as the result of it accidentally saves the life of Athen's most famous hero. Immobilized by his wound, Socrates devotes himself to meditation and becomes the wisest, as well as the most irritating, man in Greece, triumphant in spirit but infirm in the mundane world of human affairs.[8]

Other poets of the anarchic age were not always able to find such positive ways of overcoming their afflictions. Not able to cope with experience, they tried to transcend it through devotion to the ideal, recording the futile attempt with appropriate pathos. This is the wailing era of German drama, the period of extreme subjectivism, dominated by the *poeta dolorosus* and the bleeding heart, by men who measured the cost of their isolation in terms of suffering and exaltation. A particularly bad example is Hanns Johst's *Der Einsame: Ein Menschenuntergang* (*The Lonely One: The Defeat of a Human Being*), which emits a pathetic yap of self-pity for a poet whose sacrifice in the cause of humanity has gone unheeded by those for whom it was meant. I mention Johst's drama only because

8. There is a brilliant analysis of *Der gerettete Alkibiades* in Walter H. Sokel's *The Writer in Extremis*, pp. 104ff.

of its bearing on Brecht's first play. He had read *Der Einsame* and was sickened by its false pathos and sentimental
idealism. A friend dared him to do better — and he did,
offering the "dramatic biography" *Baal* (begun in 1918)
as a counter to Johst's portrait of the poet martyr, not the
poet as he would like to think of himself, but the poet as
he actually is. The anti-hero of this play has none of the
conventional graces. Neither respectable nor lily pure, he
is a great human animal bulldozing his way through life in
boozing, whoring, and brawling; a social boor and a bound-
er; seducer of other men's wives and deserter of pregnant girls, a thief, cheat, and murderer; a brigandly Dylan
of the Germanic wilderness with an insatiable lust for all
things alive. He is goalless and completely egocentric. The
only rhythms Baal knows are bodily ones, fulfilling such
elemental needs as hunger, sleep, and sex — the peristalsis
of his own physiology. His notion of an ideal activity is to
sit on the toilet, alone and at peace with himself, simultaneously gorging and eliminating, snug in the little house
man has built for himself halfway between angel and
beast. "Dies sei ein Ort," he rhapsodizes, "wo man zufrie-
den ist, / Daß drüber Sterne sind und drunter Mist." [9] The
crude physicality of these images was a little unexpected
in poetry, to be sure, but they did round out the expressionists' too-abstract view of essential man. They suggested a more universal basis for calling all men brothers
and even dropped a hint that mankind's happiness lay in
yielding himself to the ambiguous rhythms of natural existence. If life had any meaning at all, it would have to be
in using the opportunities given by earthly change.

The fictional poet of anarchy could not survive this del-
uge of vulgarity. It swept away all the sentimentality and
pathos about his calling, the notion that there was such a

9. "This is a place where one is satisfied that there are stars above and
manure below."

thing as pure spirituality or that death had a purpose beyond the termination of existence. When Baal collapses in the forest, his "spirit" expires with the body, no one mourns him and no one sees a meaning in his demise; only nature attends him with an impatient claim on his flesh and bone. The portrait Brecht draws in this first play is gross, a little crude, and sometimes repellent, yet it casts off a ghostly charm, somewhat like luminescence playing over putrefaction, the type of beauty Baudelaire and Rimbaud had introduced into lyric poetry, here transmitted into the harshly visible world of drama. The intent was clearly to rebalance a distorted view of man by overstressing those aspects which had been understressed, indulging in the negative and perverse, not as in naturalism in order to recall a "normal" or more desirable condition, but simply because these negative elements belonged to existence and because men long for something more positive.

To Brecht, as to Alfred Döblin a few years later, nature was an inseparable mixture of *Zucker und Dreck* ("sugar and filth"). Hence Baal's primitiveness, rooted in the depths of nature, in fertile earth as well as in filthy dirt, just like the trees with which he identifies. Hence, too, his futile grasping at the violet sky, which is an inspired longing even while it confirms that the heavens are not for man's dwelling. And this, too, is the reason why Baal's sexuality, although animal, is also true to instinct, an impulse to make contact in a world which has made coming together too easy and thereby robbed it of all significance. When Baal finally does experience love, it turns out to be homosexual, Brecht's way of stating perhaps, as Wedekind did before him, that the only genuine form of human communication still containing a trace of virtue lies in this essentially unfruitful type of relationship. Romanticism had turned invert.

Baal is the "real" poet of the anarchic age, in Brecht's

opinion, and he justifies the claim by putting some of the most splendid lyrics in modern German into Baal's foul mouth. The central theme of those verses is praise of the Syrian god of Earth after whom Baal is named, the embodiment of those ambivalent forces which propel life at the same time they try to destroy it. The choice was personally significant as well. For years Brecht kept a drawing of Baal in his bedroom, knowing full well the implications in feigning worship of a pagan deity whose reputation had been tarnished by the somewhat prejudiced opinion of the Hebrew prophets. Rather than pretend belief in a false idol commonly accepted as the true God, he would bow before a pagan deity commonly thought to be false because that idol still expressed a semblance of truth about the nature of man. It was clear warning that Brecht's gestures would not always point in the same direction in which he was actually going.

Brecht's next play, *Trommeln in der Nacht* (*Drums in the Night*), also written in 1918, lacks the fine frenzy of *Baal*, but carries the attack on anarchic illusions to a broader and more vulnerable audience. The play tells of a soldier home from the wars, Kragler by name, who must decide whether to stay with the woman who has betrayed him or join the Communists in creating a better world. He opts for dishonor, taking back his pregnant girl friend and turning his back on the revolution. Brecht's primary target in this *Heimkehrerdrama* was his own class, the petite bourgeoisie, and its notions about heroes and heroism. The protagonist has learned in military service that great deeds are not sufficient to halt the drift towards anarchy or to save the world from still greater anarchy ahead. He knows that the soldier is only a man after all, no better and no worse than what others make of him, and that he will continue to be used and misused by society, just like the young man in "The Legend of the Dead Soldier" with which Brecht prefaces the play, who serves his Kaiser and country until death, and then, when the need grows great again, is exhumed from the grave and pronounced fit to fight another day. Yet in spite of his knowledge that positive values cannot arise from a negative condition, Kragler elects to go on "reproducing himself so that he doesn't die out," too much the *Kleinbürger* himself not to take advantage of the opportunities peacetime offers to the experienced profiteer. His last resort is cynicism. At the end of the play he takes a drum and beats on it savagely while berating the people around him for looking at the world through romantic eyes: "Glotzt nicht so romantisch! [. . .] Ihr Halsabschneider! Ihr blutdürstige Feiglinge, ihr!"[10] And then, in an unforgettable bit of stage business, he exposes the hollow fakery of his world by hurling "die Trommel nach dem Mond, der ein Lampion war, und die Trommel und der Mond fallen in den Fluß, der kein Wasser hat."[11] The gesture is futile, of course, the frustrated outburst of a man betraying his conscience, for by his unwillingness to join the revolution Kragler knows that he has only himself to blame for the world's continuing to be as it is. In Brecht's own phrase, he has "no sense for the tragic."

Looking at *Trommeln in der Nacht* in later years, the playwright was very harsh on himself for failing to castigate his anti-hero as well as the circumstances against which Kragler is protesting. Romantic himself, and fooled by Kragler's anti-romanticism, he had chosen to end the play with the "shabbiest" of all possible variants and then had compounded the fault by letting it appear as if he agreed with Kragler's way out. Furthermore, "die Auf-

10. "Don't goggle so romantically! [. . .] You cutthroats! You bloodthirsty cowards, you!"
11. "The drum toward the moon, which was a paper lantern, and drum and moon fall into the river, which has no water."

lehnung gegen eine zu verwerfende literarische Konven-
tion führte hier beinahe zur Verwerfung einer großen so-
zialen Auflehnung." [12] Brecht knew that the drums in the
night of the title—representing the forces of historical
necessity summoning the old order to execution and the
new one to revolution—would continue to throb in spite
of Kragler and his ilk. Thus Brecht hints again that
change is inevitable and will take place whether or not
the individual willingly participates in the process.

Brecht's third play, *Im Dickicht der Städte* (*In the Jungle of the Cities*), written between 1921 and 1923, tells
how two very different men—the Malaysian timber mer-
chant, Shlink, lately of Yokohama, and Garga, a displaced
Ohioan working in a small lending library in Chicago—
become locked in a struggle without apparent motive or
purpose from which neither emerges a victor. Their story
begins on a day which is "like any other" as far as the routine of living is concerned, but totally "unlike any other"
as the opening date of their momentous struggle. Shlink
appears in the lending library with a couple of toughs,
tries to buy Garga's opinion of a book with money and the
promise of a trip to Tahiti. When he is turned down by
Garga, who protests against such "prostitution," Shlink declares the fight to be on. It rages over three years and a
few months—Brecht records the exact calendar dates—
during the course of which Shlink completely corrupts
Garga's family while Garga repeatedly brings about the
collapse of Shlink's business enterprises. The struggle ter-
minates only after both men have been destroyed: Garga
goes to prison for three years after Shlink frames him; and
Shlink, denounced by Garga for the rape of his sister, is
hounded to death by lynchers.

12. "The revolt against a literary convention which should be rejected
almost led here to the rejection of a great social revolution." Brecht,
Gesammelte Werke, 17:945.

Critics have not found it easy to make sense of this play, and Brecht has not offered them very generous assistance. His key metaphor derives from boxing, "eine der 'großen mythischen Vergnügungen der Riesenstädte von jenseits des großen Teiches,'" which he claims to have chosen merely in order to depict "'ein Kampf an sich,' ein Kampf ohne andere Ursache als den Spaß am Kampf, mit keinem anderen Ziel als der Festlegung des 'besseren Mannes' . . ." [13] In the printed version of the play, he advises the reader not to fret about the motives of the struggle but simply to watch the parry and thrust of the combatants, to judge their form without taking sides, and direct their full attention to the finish. Such advice may not be quite as cryptic as it seems. For one thing, it clearly hints at certain basic artistic goals. It seems obvious, for example, that Brecht wanted to downgrade character in favor of plot as the primary element of the play, the better to focus his audience's attention on the stages of an action or series of events rather than on the development of personality, and on the way an action might be worked out according to the premises assumed. Brecht was also concerned here with stressing the relative superiority of form over content, or at any rate with affirming that the "what" of a play is to be found in its "how." His later comments on *Im Dickicht der Städte* admit to exaggerating "das Formale" a little, "aber ich wollte darlegen, was für ein komplexes Geschäft solch ein Schreiben ist und wie das eine in das andere eingeht, wie die Formung aus dem Stofflichen kommt und auf das Stoffliche zurückschlägt." [14]

13. "One of the 'great mythical pleasures in the gigantic cities on the other side of the great pond' . . . 'a struggle in itself,' a struggle with no other cause besides the fun of fighting, with no other goal except to determine who is the 'better man' . . ." Ibid., p. 948.
14. "But I wanted to show what a complicated business such writing

The play suggests other intentions. The fight metaphor, for example, undoubtedly symbolizes a struggle between opposing forces within Brecht himself, but his choice of it may also have been made in response to the familiar anarchic problem of deteriorating human relationships. Always realistically inclined to correct someone else's errors, as we have seen, Brecht was probably trying to counter the contemporary expressionist solution (regeneration of man through ideal universal love and brotherhood) with a reminder that the real operational principle of anarchy was the law of the jungle and that communication, if indeed it is any longer possible at all, takes place only in the form of unresolved conflict — in the sadomasochistic, love-hate, homosexual type of relationship between Shlink and Garga. Shlink himself comes close to making this point in referring to their struggle as a metaphysical action and in confessing wistfully to Garga: "Die unendliche Vereinzelung des Menschen macht eine Feindschaft zum unerreichbaren Ziel [. . .] Ja, so groß ist die Vereinzelung, daß es nicht einmal einen Kampf gibt."[15] Not a conclusive fight, in any case, and this is where the play strikes hardest at the strategies of Brecht's expressionist contemporaries. What had comforted them was the assumption that even though life on earth had no inherent purpose, one could derive such a purpose from elsewhere; goal or value lay in a realm of ideas and the striving for that goal gave life meaning. The struggle in *Im Dickicht der Städte*, on the other hand, has no goal, either in itself nor beyond it, nor do the partners arrive at "Verständigung," that is, they do not reach agreement about their purpose or even come

---

is and how the one enters into the other, how form comes from subject matter and affects the subject matter in turn." Ibid., p. 950.

15. "The infinite isolation of human beings makes enmity an unreachable goal [. . .] In fact, the isolation is so great it doesn't even result in a fight."

to an understanding of each other's motives; they are as unenlightened at the end of the play as they were at the beginning. The important thing, however, is that their struggle is a process which results in fundamental change. As Brecht says, "[der Kampf hat] ihre wirtschaftliche Situation sowie sie selbst bis zur Unkenntlichkeit verändert."[16] Note that the value of this outcome is left undecided; the point is that change does take place and that struggle is its *modus operandi*. Interestingly enough, the analogy is drawn from the world of sport, implying that the struggle is a game played with deadly seriousness in order to win. It is an interaction of people and forces, involving shifting strengths and weaknesses, a series of events which alters the combatants as well as the nature of their endeavor. Thus the process is all important, even though its inner workings remain mysterious and unknown.

The turning point in Brecht's dramaturgy is the comedy *Mann ist Mann* (*Man Equals Man*), written around 1924 and first performed in Darmstadt in 1926. He wrote a number of different versions of this play, the changes instituted according to Brecht's varying ideas at the time of each new printing or production. When he took a look at the play before its inclusion in the first collection of *Stücke*, he confessed to rereading it "mit besonderen Befürchtungen,"[17] perhaps because he had forgotten how audacious the original play was, perhaps because he wondered how audiences might still respond to the play's mixture of absurdity and horror. *Mann ist Mann* tells of the transformation of the gentle stevedore Galy Gay into Jeraiah Jip, the human fighting machine. The time is 1925;

---

16. "[The struggle has] changed their economic situation, as well as themselves, almost beyond recognition." *Gesammelte Werke*, 17:971.
17. "With particular trepidation." Ibid., p. 951.

the place Kilkoa, India. Leaving his hut one morning to
buy a fish for supper, Galy Gay encounters three machine
gunners in Her (sic) Majesty's Imperial Army who have
just lost the fourth man in their unit. (He had got his hair
caught in a doorframe while robbing a pagoda and
couldn't get it loose.) Desperate for a replacement before
roll call, the soldiers beg Galy Gay to substitute for the
missing crewman, and because he is a man who can
never say no — and an opportunist to boot, with a sharp
nose for a good deal — they are able to buy his services
for the price of a few beers and a box of cigars. After roll
call, the soldiers have no further use for the little stevedore. But the next day, because their buddy Jeraiah has
apparently deserted them (the priests have actually
bribed him to remain in the pagoda and have then turned
him into a god), the soldiers decide to enlist Galy Gay
permanently as number four man in the crew. Although
he resists them at first they are able to trap him with a
ruse, and by lunch time Galy Gay has denied his identity,
held a funeral oration over his own grave, and has taken
over the name and nature of Jeraiah Jip. When the army
marches off, then, to engage in the next campaign, Galy
Gay is with them, geared for battle and soon to become
the pride of the army by leading the machine gun crew to
bloody victory at the siege of Sir El Dchowr.

Brecht's first claim here is on the audience's credulity:
the action is ludicrous, the setting an India not even Kip-
ling could have believed in, and the language wondrously
strange — not quite what we understand nowadays by
Theatre of the Absurd and without its philosophical pre-
suppositions, but a recognizable forerunner in that it anticipates many of its techniques and themes.[18] Now to

18. To quote Martin Esslin, *The Theatre of the Absurd*, p. 272: "*Mann
ist Mann* anticipates the Theatre of the Absurd in its thesis that human

chide the author for this, as if things had gotten out of hand and he had come to believe in the myth he himself had created about the English-speaking world, is more than a trifle silly. Brecht put little stock in the story as such; it was, he said, merely illustrative and could be modified at will. As for his intentions, these are made reasonably, albeit indirectly, clear when he has one of his characters turn to the audience and quote him directly concerning the point of the play. Just before the soldiers undertake Galy Gay's transformation, Widow Begbick says:

> Herr Bertolt Brecht behauptet: Mann ist Mann.
> Und das ist etwas, was jeder behaupten kann.
> Aber Herr Bertolt Brecht beweist auch dann,
> Daß man mit einem Menschen beliebig viel machen kann.
> Hier wird heute abend ein Mensch wie ein Auto ummontiert,
> Ohne daß er irgend etwas dabei verliert. [. . .]
> Herr Bertolt Brecht hofft, Sie werden den Boden, auf dem Sie stehen,
> Wie Schnee unter Ihren Füßen vergehen sehen
> Und werden schon merken bei dem Packer Galy Gay,
> Daß das Leben auf Erden gefährlich sei.[19]

Those who read Brecht for the propaganda could hardly want more; here is a message loud and clear, and it seems to tell us all we need to know in order to grasp the play's meaning. Still, one wonders. Perhaps Brecht is being a little too eager to tip his hand, as if he knew that explicit-

---

nature is not a constant, and that it is possible to transform one character into another in the course of the play."

19. "Herr Bertolt Brecht claims that man equals man, and of course that's something anyone can claim. But Herr Bertolt Brecht will prove also that you can do pretty much what you will with a human being. This evening a man will be reassembled here just like an automobile without his losing a thing in the process. Herr Bertolt Brecht hopes that you will see the ground underneath your feet pass away like snow and take due note, in this example of the stevedore Galy Gay, that life on earth is dangerous.

ness would be more apt to meet with aggressive skepticism than with implicit belief. A man who knew the theatre well, Brecht was certainly aware that an audience does not want to be told everything; it wants to find out for itself. Even more, it does not want to be told *what* it should find out. And Brecht's procedure here — so frank and ingratiatingly intimate, so charmingly moralistic — pretending to provide an authoritative word on the comedy, straight from the horse's mouth, so to speak, really limits the play's meaning to one point and one source. It says in effect: This is what *I* think; this is my view as author of what's going on. And having told us this, he hopes we will put up our guard, prick up our ears, and begin to question the truth, or at least the intent, of what is being said. Rather than trying to mold audience opinion, the Widow Begbick's speech acts catalytically in trying to provoke or change opinion with respect to a matter about which most people have already made up their minds. The speech does not so much present a theme, therefore, as state a thesis or hypothesis — and a very arguable hypothesis at that.

The actual words of Widow Begbick's speech are even more challenging. The audience, she says, is going to witness the demonstration of something seemingly impossible and is supposed to accept this as proof of the proposition that there are no limits to what can be done with a man. It's a strange juxtaposition of notions — an absurdity is to be proved like a scientific experiment and a human being modified like a machine; a transformation will result in a different product even though the elements composing it will be the same as before; there will be a change *in* nature which is no change *of* nature! It doesn't ring quite true. Either Brecht is pulling our legs (and he's not above that, as I've hinted before); or he's making another one of those poetic analogies which have a habit of breaking

down when taken too seriously; or he is slyly inducing us
to think about our way of thinking, telling us that our accustomed categories of thought and feeling might not be
quite as exclusive as we have assumed them to be. Perhaps we can no longer depend, as we have always depended, on simple logic, but must think logically and il-
logically at the same time, or admit that there is a logic in
non-logic and a non-logic in logic. Perhaps we must think
not merely in terms of rational versus irrational, but in
terms both rational and irrational, as if there were a kind
of rationality in the irrational and irrationality in the rational as well. Or is this all sheer linguistic tomfoolery? In
any case, something is happening here that needs clari-
fication, and our chances of doing this correctly will hinge
on how Brecht "proves" the absurd thesis, on his demonstrating that the transformation has situational and strategic significance.

   I hope it is understood that the Widow Begbick's comparison of man to machine is not a true metaphor with
metaphysical implications. It is rather an early instance of
Brecht's famous *Verfremdungseffekt* ("alienation effect"):
that is, an attempt to present a familiar object unfamil-
iarly, in terms unusual enough to catch an audience's attention and persuade it to reconsider the meanings habit-
ually associated with it. The technique is neither original
with Brecht nor peculiar to his work. It is a specialized instance of what Kenneth Burke calls achieving a perspective-by-incongruity, an approach much used in literature
(and other disciplines as well) for arriving at the "truth"
about objects and interrelating them to other objects in
the scheme of things. As Burke describes it: "A word belongs by custom to a certain category — and by rational
planning you wrench it loose and metaphorically apply it
to a different category." Not only words are involved,
however, but whole complexes, so that in effect one aspect

of an historical situation supplies the master metaphor for the total complex. All the plays studied so far have utilized this method, in each case choosing their imagery from a sphere dominant in contemporary interest. Thus, Hauptmann reaches into the field of medicine to diagnose the ills of his age and to express his hope for restoration of a natural and healthy human condition; Wedekind takes over the vocabulary of sex and puberty to describe the essentially moral concern of a transitional age; and Kaiser borrows terms from banking in order to deal with the matter of creativity and communication in a condition of anarchy. Brecht proceeds in like manner and for similar reasons, since "perspective-by-incongruity" proves to be a highly effective way of calling a spade a spade, that is, of sizing up or gauging situations. It seems devious, but as Burke asserts, it "brings us nearest to the simple truth" about them; rather than being merely "negative smuggling," it is really "positive cards-face-up-on-the-table. It is designed to 'remoralize' by accurately naming a situation already demoralized by inaccuracy." [20] In making the comparison of man to machine, therefore, or in describing the contemporary situation in images derived from war and the military, Brecht was simply trying to deal with historical reality on its own terms, war and machinery being instances of scientific thought applied technologically, developments which had captured — and alarmed — the imagination in that era.

The transformation of Galy Gay takes place in five steps, the first four comprising the ruse by which the soldiers trap him into denying his identity, the last one centering on his burial, funeral oration and rebirth as Jeraiah Jip. Each step of the action is numbered, and the earlier ones are preceded by a title phrase indicating what is

20. Kenneth Burke, *Attitudes towards History*, pp. 308–9.

about to take place. The setting is a canteen belonging to the Widow Begbick, a purveyor of extramilitary supplies and supplier of paramilitary needs, who is herself an active participant in the action and occasionally comments upon it. In particular, she interrupts the proceedings every so often to sing another verse of her song, *Vom Fluß der Dinge* ("About the Fluidity of Things"), the theme of which is that man's existence is like standing in the water: the element itself is constant, but what constitutes it varies; therefore one should never hope to hold (the German word in this context is also ambiguous) to what is there:

> Beharre nicht auf der Welle
> Die sich an deinem Fuß bricht, solange er
> Im Wasser steht, werden sich
> Neue Wellen an ihm brechen.[21]

Step number one is entitled *Das Elefantengeschäft* ("The Elephant Deal") and the title phrase runs: "Die MG.-Abteilung überreicht dem Mann, der nicht genannt sein will, einen Elefanten." [22] In this scene, basing their tactics on the elephant's great prestige in India and on Galy Gay's inability to turn down a good deal, the soldiers persuade him to sell an elephant for them anonymously in exchange for a share in the profits. The customer is the Widow Begbick and the object of the sale is an unregistered beast, allegedly from army surplus, who answers to the name Billy Humph. (He is actually an artificial monstrosity formed by stretching a piece of canvas over the bodies of two soldiers crouching underneath.) Galy Gay notes how he had set out that morning to buy a fish but

21. "Don't hold to the wave which breaks at your foot; as long as it is in the water new waves will break upon it."
22. "The machine gun crew hands over an elephant to the man who wants to remain anonymous."

now has an elephant. This rise in his fortunes encourages him to overlook any possible deception, and concluding that his mother must have been right when she told him that "one can't know anything for sure," he agrees to act as seller for the beast.

Step number two is *Die Elefantenauktion* ("The Elephant Auction"): "Der Mann, der nicht genannt sein will, verkauft den Elefanten."[23] In this scene Galy Gay declares himself publicly to be the rightful owner of the beast and satisfies his own doubts about its genuineness. "Da er gekauft wird, habe ich keinen Zweifel . . . Elefant ist Elefant, besonders wenn er gekauft wird."[24] The elephant seems to be healthy since it urinates promptly on cue, so Galy Gay auctions off Billy Humph, as his own property, to the Widow Begbick. The moment he receives her check, however, the soldiers seize him, accusing him of dealing in stolen goods. And when the canvas falls off, exposing the beast as a fake, the Widow adds the charge that she has been tricked into entering a fraudulent transaction. Galy Gay is arrested. Meanwhile the Widow advises him (and the audience) in another song not to take any name, an elephant's or one's own, too seriously.

> Nenne doch nicht so genau deinen Namen. Wozu denn?
> Wo du doch immerzu einen andern damit nennst.
> Und wozu so laut deine Meinung, vergiß sie doch.
> Welche war es denn gleich? Erinnere dich doch nicht
> Eines Dinges länger, als es selber dauert.[25]

23. "The man who wants to remain anonymous sells the elephant."
24. "Since it's to be sold I don't have any doubts. An elephant's an elephant, especially when it's sold."
25. "Don't be so sure of your name. What for, anyway? Since you always mean someone else when you use it. Why express your opinion so loudly? Just forget it. What was it, by the way? Don't think about anything longer than it lasts."

Step number three in Galy Gay's transformation is *Der Prozeß gegen den Mann, der nicht genannt sein will* ("The trial of the man who wants to remain anonymous"). In this scene the elephant salesman, who according to witnesses wore a beard and was called Galy Gay, is threatened with death. When he hears this, the little stevedore insists he can't be the man they are looking for because his name is not Galy Gay. He also denies that he might be the missing Jeraiah Jip, as the soldiers suggest. "Einer ist keiner," [26] he remarks sagely, and while he sits there trying to make up his mind, the Widow Begbick warns him in another song that "of all certain things, the most certain by far is doubt." He asks her then to fetch him a scissors in order to cut off his beard, thereby doing away as he thinks with the last bit of incriminating evidence.

Step number four is *Die Erschießung des Galy Gay in den Militärbaracken zu Kilkoa* ("The execution of Galy Gay in the military barracks at Kilkoa"). Betrayed by the Widow Begbick, who tells the soldiers about his having shaved off his beard, Galy Gay is read the charges condemning him to death. "Höre gut zu, Mann, erstens, weil du einen Elefanten der Armee gestohlen und verkauft hast, was ein Diebstahl ist, zweitens weil du einen Elefanten verkauft hast, der kein Elefant war, was ein Betrug ist, und drittens, weil du keinerlei Namen noch Paß zeigen kannst und vielleicht sogar ein Spion bist, was Landesverrat ist." [27] At this point Galy Gay is ready to swear that his name is Jeraiah Jip. Nevertheless, he is placed against the wall and the countdown begins. At two comes the great

26. "Someone is as good as no one."
27. "Prick up your ears, man! First, because you stole and sold an army elephant, which is theft; second, because you sold an elephant that wasn't an elephant, which is fraud; third, because you have neither a name nor a passport and are perhaps even a spy, which is treason."

confession. "Ich gestehe, daß ich nicht weiß, was mit mir
geschehen ist. Glaubt mir und lacht nicht, ich bin einer,
der nicht weiß, wer er ist. Aber Galy Gay bin ich nicht, das
weiß ich. Der erschoßen werden soll, bin icht nicht.
Wer aber bin ich? [. . .] So ihr einen findet, der vergessen
hat, wer er ist, das bin ich." [28] That's all the soldiers
need, and with the cry: "Einmal ist keinmal," [29] they fire
their blanks at the wretched little fellow and he falls over
in a dead faint.

The second part of the transformation, announced as
step number five, is *Leichenbegängnis und Grabrede des
Galy Gay* ("The burial and funeral oration of Galy Gay").
The soldiers fetch an enormous box, chalk their victim's
name on its side, awaken the "corpse," and give him something to eat. Almost certain now that the little stevedore is
no more since he recalls being at his execution, Galy Gay
ruminates for a moment at the coffin, explaining to himself
why he won't check inside in order to be sure as to who, if
anyone, is lying within. How does a man really know who
he is, he asks; does one part of him recognize another
part? does either part know it belongs to the same person?
and if a man is not his own mother's son, as he believes,
nevertheless he must be some mother's son, so what's the
difference? "Einer ist keiner," he concludes: "es muß ihn
einer anrufen. [. . .]"

Und ich, der eine ich und der andere ich
Werden gebraucht und sind also brauchbar.
Und hab' ich nicht angesehen diesen Elefanten
Drück ich ein Auge zu, was mich betrifft

28. "I confess that I don't know what's happened to me. Believe me
and don't laugh, I'm someone who doesn't know who he is. But I'm not
Galy Gay — I know that. And I'm not the man who's supposed to be shot.
But who am I? [. . .] If you find someone who's forgotten who he is,
that'll be me."
29. "Once is as good as never."

Und lege ab, was unbeliebt an mir, und bin
Da angenehm.[30]

One is, then, as one is "called"; it all depends on serving a
need, on being used and being useful. So rationalizing,
and convinced that he is Jeraiah because the soldiers call
and treat him accordingly, Galy Gay holds a eulogy over
his own grave and marches off, with his new identity, to
war.

The absurd has a way of eluding simple statement, and
it seemed prudent to review these events thoroughly before speculating about what Brecht might be trying to say
here. Most striking, in all of this, is the head-on approach
to the problem of change. In the plays discussed previously, change is thematic and, initially at least, external
to the action — a background force making itself known
primarily through its effects on the characters or their situation. Only with *Von morgens bis mitternachts* is the
kind of change being talked about actually integrated
with what is going on on stage. *Mann ist Mann* takes this
dialectical development a step further, for here the action
involves a concrete instance of change which is itself
placed under radical scrutiny. Not only are theme and
subject matter joined, but together they become an issue
for open debate.

Other differences are equally significant. In *Einsame
Menschen*, for example, Hauptmann concentrates on the
circumstantial aspects of change, grounding it in actual
historical conditions and registering its effects on the individual's way of life. The problems of Hauptmann's play
come out of external events, and the solution the charac-

30. "One is as good as no one until someone calls him. And I, the one
self and the other self, are useful and therefore usable. And if I didn't look
at this elephant, I can disregard what concerns me, take off what people
don't like about me, and then just be a pleasant fellow."

ters long for is *Anderswerden*: a different state of affairs
or other personal circumstances than those at hand. No
one was very hopeful about things "becoming otherwise,"
however, for according to the cause-and-effect mentality
of the time, every event was determined by prior events
and human nature was powerless to bring about changes
on its own. Hence the demoralization of Hauptmann's
lonely men and women: their fragmented psyche, isolation from the prevailing system of pieties, moral paralysis,
and general confusion as to purpose or goals. Theirs was a
static condition within a time of transition. Suspended between what they were no longer a part of and what they
were not able to become, they were in a particularly ironic
situation (or tragically ironic), at odds with their own conviction that evolution was taking place throughout existence, in society as well as in nature. Although they had to
participate in the process of change, willy-nilly, they would
not draw any benefits themselves from its eventual consequences. In spite of Hauptmann's objectivity in depicting
this condition, his interpretation of it as a true dilemma
suggests that he identified even more closely with his hap-
less-helpless protagonist than is generally acknowledged.
His explanation why Johannes fails to act, in spite of his
superior talents and knowledge of conditions, was in fact
a means of unburdening his own badly troubled conscience. Hence a strategy based on the principles of conventional tragedy; he calls for resignation. Having been
satisfied by the logic of causes and effects that the present
state of affairs was inevitable, and, for the moment at
least, irreparable, Hauptmann could accept the situation
in good conscience, dignifying his defeat with vicarious
compassion for those unlucky enough to suffer because of
the same situation, hoping against hope that society might
somehow be moved to look for a means of bettering conditions in the future.

Writing in the same period of transition, Wedekind also experienced change in relationship to conscience, but with a different personal burden. Where Hauptmann needed to rationalize his *not* having acted, Wedekind was constrained to justify his having acted as he did; Hauptmann had to account to himself for avoiding a confrontation with circumstances, Wedekind to invent good reasons for continuing to exploit its possibilities as he wished. And Wedekind was successful largely because he found a more accommodating notion about the nature of change. He realized that the critical moments of history are recurrent in life, that they were not occasioned by accidental circumstances, but rather inherent in the very process of living as men continually leave one state and enter into another. That transitional process is beautifully symbolized in *Frühlingserwachen* by puberty. Now Wedekind knew that changes in nature are not in themselves problematic; they become so only because human beings believe they must try to cope with such changes in terms of a prevailing moral system — hence the wrong-headedness of conventional tragedy, in which the inevitable outcome is the triumph of universal order at the cost of individual destruction. Wedekind would have no part of this. He insisted that life — and by this he meant actual physical existence — is the only scene and rationale of human actions. To make living possible without incurring the risk of guilt, he formulated a definition of morality according to which the individual struggling to realize himself can, in effect, scarcely do wrong. The magic is contained in that formula which defines morality as the real product of imaginary factors; it is what one must reckon with after calculating the interaction between what one is supposed to do (*Sollen*) and what one's own nature prompts one to do (*Wollen*). The solution is a simple matter of reevaluating the elements one has to deal with in life so that they can be manipulated in a way most advantageous to one-self. This strategy has close affinities with humor, of course, for it is based on a good-natured shrug-of-the-shoulder recognition of facts, among others that any transition entails the death of something no longer viable. Essentially it is a technique of rationalization, for it explains situations in terms that preclude one's actions from ever getting one down, least of all by burdening one's conscience. The strategy acquires a kind of absolute sanctity, furthermore, through Wedekind's equating his own nature with Nature, for from this he derived the purpose and direction of his life. He could excuse his actions as an inevitable and therefore irreproachable response to Nature's demands. He knew that the individual armed with such an attitude would not be shaken by any change in circumstances and that its worst effects could do no more than throw him temporarily off balance. By this elastic mental stance he would be protected from any real damage.

The problem for Kaiser was quite different. In a period of anarchy there seemed to be no possibility of fundamental change, either in the rationalized world of social institutions or in the haphazard world of mundane experience. These worlds were full of motion, but without real movement, circles of repetitive activity with no purpose beyond that inherent in the activity itself. The question, then, was how to supplant the motion with valid motivation, so that a meaning could be found within the apparent meaninglessness and the circle of errors be turned into a cycle of significant change. Needed was a sense of "end" or goal which would imbue one's actions with consequence and therefore make them appear worthwhile. Kaiser found his answer in redefining contemporary meanings and the nature of the ways in which one arrives at them. It was a step further in the direction pointed out by Wedekind, but where the strategy of reformulation aims only at assigning arbitrary values to events in order to cope with them on one's own terms, Kaiser's dialectical strategy uses linguistic means to transform the nature of events themselves. In the interaction between things and their potentiality, objects become what they are. Words are the symbolic instruments for accomplishing this, of course, and using them to create new meanings becomes the purpose of Kaiser's activity.

In shifting from the problem of change to the process of exchange, Kaiser laid a new foundation for the development of strategies in German drama. Significantly, he diverted attention from circumstances to relationships, from actual events to the connections between them and their ideal possibilities. Value was no longer ascribed to any thing as such, to its qualities or even its psychological effects, but rather to its usefulness as an instrument for achieving certain results. In stressing a goal or end for one's actions, Kaiser rejected the cause-and-effect determinism of an earlier age in favor of the teleological point of view; acts are not merely the result of prior events, they are also initiatory steps toward a desired future. The Vision, in other words, made it possible for men to think of themselves again as creators and to devise strategies for remaking the world according to their ideal image of its essential nature.

Like other expressionist strategies, Kaiser's shares qualities both "scientific" and "romantic." It is scientific in its emphasis on functionalism and instrumentality, and on the process of abstraction by which we arrive at meaning; it is romantic in its longing for possibilities without working out the actual means and methods by which they might be realized. Kaiser himself seems content to remain within the area of dialectic divorced from any real connections with nature or experience. His Kassierer dies *to* this world *for the sake of* this world, but in doing so is no longer in or part of it, withdrawing, like Kaiser himself, from all active participation — apart from the intellectual — in order to devote himself utterly to his medium.

None of this was lost on the early Brecht, who, for all his generous (and generously acknowledged) borrowing from Kaiser, could not stomach what he considered the latter's almost puritanical abstinence from real life.[31] Like all the dramatists before him, Kaiser had disregarded the positive opportunity offered by change for altering the relationships between men and reconstructing the conditions of their physical existence. Even Wedekind, in spite of his eager submission to the processes of nature, kept a wary eye on change as an ever possible threat to his equilibrium. Brecht, on the other hand, from the outset, welcomes change in any guise. Baal models his life on the rhythms of nature and is guided by the ups and downs of his own metabolism; Kragler bows to the inevitability of historical change even while refusing to assist in bringing it about; Shlink and Garga, driven by irrational urges to their "metaphysical" struggle, discover through their involvement with each other that they, and their situation, are changed "almost beyond recognition." In *Mann ist Mann*, change is explicitly acclaimed as the inevitable concomitant of existence and the characteristic aspect of man's condition. As the Widow Begbick constantly reminds the audience, it is a fact of experience which, precisely because it is potentially disastrous, offers a challenge to investigation and calls forth our best efforts to manipulate it. A problem, of course, but a problem not

31. He may have been wrong about this, at least in one respect, for although Kaiser was never publicly or politically active there is some evidence of his having lived a life full of private — and ultimately frustrating — complications. I strongly suspect that Kaiser's condemnation of his protagonist's search for value in the mundane world is a case of sour grapes; more success in his own attempt at experience would have done away with the necessity to compensate through the intricacies of dialectic.

to be eluded, or overcome, or escaped from, or even intellectualized — but rather, one to be faced squarely with the aim of gaining the upper hand. Since all things in nature change, it may be assumed that man is also changeable and capable of being changed, capable even of changing himself. For Brecht the issue is not whether one can attain peace of mind by altering circumstances or adjusting oneself to them, since these like oneself are in constant flux; not whether one can adopt a more flexible attitude to events in order to deal with them as one wills, since problems continue to exist regardless of one's disposition to them; and certainly not whether one can find new motives for one's actions in an absolute realm apart from experience, since such motivation was irrelevant to the processes of nature and without any bearing on its outcome. The issue, as Brecht sees it, is much more pragmatic; it is a matter of sizing up situations in terms of flux, of tracing the course of events by which change manifests itself, and then of gauging the possibilities (including those in human nature itself) for alteration. In short, the problem of change, measured by its effects, becomes the problem of method — of selecting the proper means for controlling the direction of change in order to bring about the results one desires.

Brecht's position is implicit in his choice of the word *Verwandlung* to designate the transformations in *Mann ist Mann*, and it may be advisable at this point to consider the implications of that term. Unlike *Anderswerden*, the transitionist's word for change, or *Wandlung*, the anarchist's designation for inner conversion or a basic change of attitude, *Verwandlung* usually denotes a phenomenal or functional transformation without implying any natural or substantive process. The term is used most frequently in the sciences. In metallurgy, for example, *Verwandlung* describes the transmutation of one element into another; in mathematics the changing of configurations; in commerce the convertibility of one kind of goods into another, and so forth. All these changes involve a rearrangement of parts or a new relationship among given factors — transitive changes by which something moves from one kind of phenomenal or functional existence to another. Similarly, the term *Verwandlung* is used in magic — which is, after all, a primitive kind of science — to indicate the manipulation by which objects are replaced by or transformed into other objects; and in the theater to describe the change of identity by which an actor takes on a role, or the process of shifting scenery to indicate a different setting or scene. Here again the term always signifies a physical or external change, the results of which are not always distinguishable from what existed previously — a change in conditions to accompany a change in function, without altering the basic elements involved. The actor remains the same man however many roles he plays; the stage remains the same place however many locations it is made to represent.

Brecht takes great pains to stress these connotations of the word, especially in the transformation of Galy Gay. While the soldiers are working on him, for example, the actual physical setting in which their action takes place is being dismantled. Piece by piece, the boards and canvas which make up the Widow Begbick's canteen are removed, washed, folded up, and stored away, just like Galy Gay, ready for future use. For later productions of the play, Brecht underscored the physicality of the transformation even more by suggesting the use of masks to mark its various stages.[32]

Now in employing the term *Verwandlung* for what happens in *Mann ist Mann*, Brecht had something of extraor-

32. Brecht, "Anmerkungen zum Lustspiel *Mann ist Mann*," *Gesammelte Werke*, 17:980ff. See especially p. 986.

dinary historical significance in mind and wanted his audiences to be well aware of it. In the scene immediately
preceding the elephant ruse, he has Jesse Mahoney, one of
the machine gun crew, turn to the Widow Begbick and
explain sententiously what the soldiers are about to do
and why their transformation should be regarded as *ein
historisches Ereignis* ("an historic event").

Die Persönlichkeit wird unter die Lupe genommen, dem
Charakterkopf wird nähergetreten. Es wird durchgegriffen.
Die Technik greift ein. [. . .] Die Persönlichkeit! Schon die
alten Assyrier, Witwe Begbick, stellten die Persönlichkeit dar
als einen Baum, der sich entfaltet. So, entfaltet! Dann wird er
eben wieder zugefaltet, Witwe Begbick. Was sagt Kopernikus? Was dreht sich? Die Erde dreht sich. Die Erde, also der
Mensch. Nach Kopernikus. Also daß der Mensch nicht in der
Mitte steht. Jetzt schauen Sie sich das einmal an. Das soll in
der Mitte stehen? Historisch ist das. Der Mensch ist gar
nichts! Die Moderne Wissenschaft hat nachgewiesen, daß
alles relativ ist. [. . .] Der Mensch steht in der Mitte, aber
nur relativ.[33]

What interests us first in this speech — apart from the fact
that it is spoken by an unlettered soldier — is the blunt
declaration that our notions of character and personality
no longer have any real meaning or validity. Jesse's scorn
of these concepts is scathing. Somewhat earlier in the

33. "This personality will now be put under the microscope, this face,
so expressive of character, will now be observed more closely. Drastic
measures will be taken. Technology will take over. [. . .] Personality!
The Assyrians, Widow Begbick, had already looked upon personality as a
tree that unfolds. So, unfolds! Then we'll just fold it up again, Widow
Begbick! What does Copernicus say? What revolves? The earth revolves.
The earth, therefore man. According to Copernicus. That means that man
doesn't stand in the center of things. Now just look at that one. And he's
supposed to be at the center of things? Historical, that's what he is. Man
is nothing, nothing at all. Modern science has proved that everything is
relative. [. . .] Man stands at the center of things, but only relatively."

play, he had spoken in even plainer soldier-fashion: "Mich kann man auch am Arsch lecken mit Charakterköpfen!"[34] And when the soldiers finally "execute" the former stevedore, they are certain they have done away with the "letzte Charakterkopf im Jahre neunzehnhunderfünfundzwanzig."[35]

Now the notions under attack here are the ones which had prevailed in German thought ever since Goethe's famous formulation of them over a century and a half earlier. Personality, according to the Goethean view, is a "gift of nature," the elemental energy bestowed on an individual at birth which distinguishes him from all other creatures. It is the core of a man's being, the thing that makes him uniquely himself, and is identical with the self or the self's innermost nature, the essential or unifying element among the complex aggregate of accidental factors making up a man's life. Personality always exists *in potentia,* according to Goethe, as something to be developed in the course of a lifetime and whose attainment brings "supreme happiness to the children of this earth." It is "subject to organic growth from within and to interference from without," undergoing multiple morphological variations in the process of self-realization. Yet, in spite of the many aspects it takes on, the essence of personality never changes: it remains as given and unfolds only in the direction determined by its own nature, very much like a flower whose eventual form is already contained in the seed. "Geprägte Form, die lebend sich entwickelt," is Goethe's celebrated phrase for it, and to this he adds the comment that an individual basically never changes.[36]

---

34. "And as far as these guys of character are concerned, you can kiss my ass too."

35. "The last guy with character in the year 1925."

36. "Distinctive form, which develops as it lives." Goethe, "Urworte. Orphisch," *Daimon. Werke,* 41:215. (Weimar, 1887–1920)

Jesse alludes directly to the Goethean view when he suggests that *entfalten* ("unfold") has been replaced by the notion of *zufalten* ("fold up"), a word normally reserved for such physical objects as paper or cloth.

Closely related to personality is character, for it is "that constellation of qualities by which the individual personality becomes manifest." In Goethe's own maxim, "Charakter im großen und kleinen ist, daß der Mensch demjenigen eine stete Folge gibt, dessen er sich fähig fühlt." It is the individual's ability to preserve the unity of his self by following the directional law of his own nature. Goethe concedes that the term is usually reserved for great or strong men, but insists that even a coward or a weakling may show character, "bis zum Wurm hinunter, der sich krümmt, wenn er getreten wird," as long as he is willing to give up those things which "andere Menschen über alles schätzen, was aber nicht zu seiner Natur gehört: die Ehre, den Ruhm, nur damit er seine Persönlichkeit erhalte." Thus character manifests itself in a man's actions and deeds, and in that sense is the same as his life's history. It is the flesh and blood record of his attempts to realize the potential of personality within the limits of the cultural environment and of his own biological-physiological makeup.[37]

In Goethe's conception, character and personality are substantive, that is, they belong to a given order of nature, itself permanent and fundamentally unchanging, and they exist in their own right with no other function than to be

37. "In great as well as in little things, character means that a human being always responds to what he feels himself capable of. . . . down to the worm which writhes when stepped on. . . . other men value above all else, but which do not belong to his own nature: honor, fame — just to preserve his personality" [translation by Arnold Bergstraesser]. A good summary of Goethe's views is given in Bergstraesser, *Goethe's Image of Man and Society*, chap. 1.

themselves.[38] When a man strives to fulfill his personality, therefore, he is attempting to realize an end which in essence is already set for him in the nature of things. And this end, this "ideal" condition, is held to be the only true or "real" state, anything short of it being merely an untidy state of affairs, something one has to remove, overcome, or alter, as the case might be, in order to reach the fundamental reality which alone would give life meaning. The changes of life, whether within or without as part of the historical process, are always inimical to the realization of that ideal state. Hence in the pre-Brechtian plays we studied, the dramatic problem arises when an individual finds his way to self-fulfillment thwarted. The action, in turn, revolves around an individual's efforts to meet this challenge, and through this test of his character, to realize his potential personality. Each protagonist faces a different set of obstacles. For Johannes Vockerat, the obstacle lies in moral or social circumstances, hence his longing to alter these or himself and become something other than what circumstances would make of him; for Melchior Gabor the obstacle is an outmoded system of pieties, hence his adoption of an attitude which will allow him to act as his own nature dictates; and for Kassierer it is the persistence of an orientation or motivation that he must replace or reinterpret in order to find something of fundamental value.

These pre-Brechtian protagonists do not, of course, accomplish their aim. How could they, indeed, since the problems as posed would permit no solutions short of terminating living itself. Thus, the assumption of a substantive reality, presupposing as it does that reality lies in something fundamentally unchanging, rules out the possibility of remaking the conditions under which life must be

---

38. Walter H. Sokel, *The Writer in Extremis*, pp. 116f. The text discussion which follows is indebted to Sokel's lucid distinctions.

lived so that they will conform to man's needs or desires. This failure calls for some sort of compensation, and in fact the strategies devised by Hauptmann, Wedekind, and Kaiser are all, in one sense, compensatory: they comfort the human psyche for its inability to control or dominate nature. Such a view must have always been intolerable to the nontragic mind. In the latter part of the nineteenth century it came to seem untenable as well, for as modern technology, accompanied by rapid changes in all forms of life, showed increasing ability to modify physical nature, it became more and more difficult to believe in a self-contained, already created, and permanent natural order. The Goethean view began to give way before a radically different conception of nature and its operations. Following the lead of physics, which had exposed matter as a bundle of energy, nature was now thought to consist of conglomerate discrete phenomena, held together by electrical forces and identified by the manner in which their various elements were related to each other. Not substance, but function became the key to reality, and order was interpreted not in terms of a fixed pattern within an already existing whole, but in terms of the particular way in which parts or events were arranged to form an operative structure. Psychology soon picked up the clue given by physics and began investigating the agents which lay at the base of men's actions, replacing the notion of character with the notion of behavior, and the idea of an innate personality with the idea of a personality defined by what an individual does and how he relates to other things. "The core of personality is no longer assumed to exist; only the processes, the 'pure form' of its manifestation, are granted a degree of reality."[39] Human nature, in

39. Ibid., p. 116. The example Sokel cites, and from which he frequently quotes, is the work of Gottfried Benn.

other words, was regarded as coextensive with physical nature and was assumed to have similar characteristics. Both are ambivalent and multipotential, and both exist as a structure of relationships whose pattern, in every individual case, is determined by the sequence in which actions or events take place. The new view provided a convincing solution to the old problem of whether or not human nature itself is capable of change. The answer was both yes and no. Human nature does not change in the sense that men will always be men and have certain characteristics — for example, the necessity to act — which they must exhibit in order to qualify as human beings; human nature does change, however, inasmuch as individual men can and do act in different ways at different times, the difference in behavior making in effect a difference in the man.[40]

It is easy to detect this viewpoint in *Mann ist Mann.* Widow Begbick states explicitly, when she tries to entice Sergeant Fairchild into spending the night with her, that nature, and therefore human beings, are basically ambivalent and contradictory. "Komm," she cajoles him,

> Zu mir in dieser Nacht des lauen Regens
> Genau wie du befürchtest: als Mensch!
> Als Widerspruch. Als Muss-und-will-doch-nicht.
> Jetzt komm als Mensch! So wie Natur dich schuf
> Ganz ohne Eisenhut! Verwirrt und wild und in dich selbst
>   verwickelt
> Und unbewehrt gegeben deinen Trieben
> Und hilflos deiner eigenen Stärke hörig.
> So komm: als Mensch![41]

40. See Kenneth Burke, *The Philosophy of Literary Form*, p. 85n.
41. "Come to me in this night of gentle rain just as you fear: as a human being! As a contradiction. As you-have-to-and-don't-want-to. Come now as a human being. Just as nature created you, without your helmet. Confused and wild and entangled in yourself and given over defenselessly to

Now from what happens to Fairchild, Brecht seems to be saying that this inner contradictory aspect of human nature is to be feared since it can be the cause of man's undoing. The sergeant does yield to the widow, surrendering to his irrepressible sexuality, and is as a consequence reduced to weak-kneed helplessness, a drivelling snivelling creature despised by her as well as by his own men. The irony is that the quality in which he takes most pride is the one to which he is also most susceptible, and that his insistence on proving his prowess becomes the cause of his powerlessness.

So it is with the play's other transformations. The process of change follows the path of least resistance, beginning at the point where a human, all-too-human trait gets the upper hand. Thus Jeraiah Jip, who, as his buddies believe, could not be held back by "ten horses" from rejoining them, is persuaded by the temple priests to remain in the pagoda and function as their living god because a "small piece of horse flesh," delivered promptly at meal times, is sufficient to satisfy his prodigious appetite for food and drink. And Galy Gay, proud of not being able to say no, or of never overlooking a good business deal, falls naturally for the soldiers' elephant ruse. As they say, "So einer verwandelt sich ganz von selber," [42] meaning that it is a quality in his own nature which accounts for the change he eventually undergoes. The transformations, then, are realignments of the elements within one's nature according to the possibilities in use. Galy Gay as Jeraiah Jip both is and is not the same man — the same physical being as before, an entity made up of the same elements; yet not the same because the arrangement of those elements, the way in which they function as shown in his be-

---

your own urges and helplessly submissive to your own strength. So come: as a human being."

42. "That kind of guy actually changes all by himself."

havior and actions, is radically different. The change resides, of course, in how he serves a need, in the way he
relates to others or in the use to which others put him.
And since a man is known by such relationships and by
his behavior, so will he be designated, the name signifying
both who and what he is. Galy Gay becomes what is made
of him; he is known through the uses to which he is put.
He is, ultimately, what he is doing, and his identity is
formed by what or whom he belongs to.

All this Brecht has symbolized by the elephant image.
When Galy Gay leaves home that fateful morning to buy
himself a fish for supper, his wife tells him scornfully: "Du
bist wie ein Elefant, der das schwerfälligste Tier der
Tierwelt ist,"[43] a clumsy and docile creature. Yet she immediately adds: "Aber er läuft wie ein Güterzug, wenn er
ins Laufen kommt,"[44] a raging, rampaging beast. And so
it is. At the beginning of the play, Galy Gay is easygoing,
placid and pliable, always ready to do someone a good
turn, good-natured and passive. This is how the soldiers
find him. "Die Stimme seines Weibes erschreckte ihn.
Ohne Führung war er nicht imstande, einen Fisch zu kaufen. Für eine Zigarre war er bereit, den Namen seines Va-
ters zu vergessen."[45] But at the end of the play, rising to
his potentiality, Galy Gay becomes as his wife has suggested, an animal run amok, totally indifferent to what
it runs over, without scruple or without guilt, a
thoroughly rationalized brute, "unaufhaltsam wie ein
Kriegselefant."[46] The image tells us that he contains in
himself the extreme range of "elephant" behavior, display-

43. "You're like an elephant, the most ponderous animal in the whole
animal world."
44. "But it runs like a freight train once it gets into motion."
45. "The voice of his wife frightened him. Without guidance he wasn't
capable of buying a fish. For a cigar, he was ready to forget the name of
his own father."
46. "No more to be held back than a war elephant."

ing the one or the other according to the situation, rising and falling to the possibilities in his own nature.

Galy Gay's transformation raises two interrelated problems: why Brecht should elect to depict a change from gentle stevedore to human fighting machine, and why the soldiers should be the agents for accomplishing it. Objections to the direction of change have been notably strong, in part because it is difficult to see anything positive in the negative process, in part because the soldiers' procedure recalls more painful matters of recent history. As Esslin and many others have remarked, their methods do "foreshadow the brainwashing techniques of totalitarian society" with uncannily prophetic accuracy.[47] One way of accounting for Brecht's choice is to assume that he created this example as a warning — not necessarily of future occurrences, but of the dire consequences in permitting one's self to be taken advantage of. After all, Galy Gay is not entirely innocent of his own undoing. By his drift and complacency, by letting others run over him, he makes himself an easy prey for the predatory minded, just as his interest in personal gain causes him to overlook the trap being laid for him. A man who can't say no is apt to become a yes-man for anything; a man who wants to remain anonymous might have to accept the name someone else wants to impose upon him. According to this line of reasoning, the play is a warning to the gentler ones among us that we should not let others do unto us what we would not dream of doing unto them.

There may be some truth in this interpretation, although it would be unfortunate to push it to the point of assuming Brecht means that people who are most imposed upon have only themselves to blame for the evils to which they are subjected — a notion rather too prevalent in our

47. Martin Esslin, *Brecht: The Man and His Work*, p. 252.

day, I fear, and all too comforting to many of us even
without the cushioning statistics assembled to support it.
In any case, the interpretation might be hard to maintain,
for as Eric Bentley points out, "The fable of brainwashing
is combined . . . with one that contradicts it: the fable of
a sorcerer's apprentice or Frankenstein's monster."[48] He is
referring to the original, full-length version of the play in
which Galy Gay is shown beating the machine gun crew
at its own game: the would-be victim, demanding his
buddies' food for himself, eventually becomes lord over
his own victimizers. Besides, this interpretation lacks the
author's backing. Although Brecht allows the Widow Begbick to quote him about the dangers of being compla-
cently smug, none of his later comments indicate that this
was most on his mind. Thus in 1927 his major concern was
how audiences would interpret the figure of Galy Gay. He
rebukes those who looked upon the protagonist as a weakling and who deplored the soldiers' action as playing
around with the stevedore and then forcing him to surrender "sein kostbares Ich, sozusagen das einzige, was er
besitzt."[49] But this is no loss, according to Brecht. On the
contrary, Galy Gay enjoys an advantage in being so
adaptable and actually gains through the transformation
by becoming "stronger" as a member of the "masses."
His great talent, Brecht says, is his opportunism: "Und
ein Mensch, der eine solche Haltung einnimmt, muß
gewinnen."[50]

That this opinion reflects a growing attachment to
Marxism, and the attendant idea of collective action, is
undeniable. (The following year Brecht began attending

48. "On Brecht's *In the Swamp, A Man's a Man* and *Saint Joan of the
Stockyards,*" Peter Demetz, ed., *Brecht: A Collection of Critical Essays,*
p. 55.
49. "His precious ego, so to speak the only thing he owns."
50. "And a man who takes such an attitude is bound to win."

lectures at the Marxist Workers' College in Berlin.) Less
obvious is its strategic intent. As usual in these earliest
years, Brecht aims at the negative in the hope of hitting
the positive. By discrediting the expressionist belief in the
superior individual and the tragedy of subjectivism, he
put his finger on integration and cohesive social action as
the more effective way of coping with the anarchic situation. The subtitle of *Mann ist Mann* describes it as a comedy, and in truth, the action does join an individual to a
social group, thereby affirming, despite its perversity, the
comic view of life. This also seems to be one point in
contrasting Galy Gay's transformation with that simultaneously going on in Sergeant Fairchild. The two transformations form a reverse parallel: Galy Gay, the innocuous
civilian, becomes a fierce warrior, while Fairchild, the ty-
rannical noncom, becomes a pitiable hanger-on; Galy Gay
achieves fame as the leader of a group, while Fairchild
loses his reputation and ability to lead men; Galy Gay
makes himself indispensable, while Fairchild is discarded
as unneeded and unnecessary. The difference lies in each
man's relative willingness (or unwillingness) to surrender
his individuality — to sacrifice his own interests and private affairs and be known by the name that signifies his
functional use to the group. Galy Gay's transformation is a
history of losing individual characteristics in the course of
attaining a social identity; Fairchild's, a history of satisfying personal desires and neglecting his duties until he has
lost place and face in the army community. At issue is a
man's potency —his effectiveness or strength or value to
others — a point fully revealed at the end of the play
through a more than heavy-handed comparison between
the two men's sexual and military prowess. Having abandoned the soldiers for a night of pleasure when they most
needed him, the sergeant forfeits the respect of his woman
as well as his men. In the futile hope of regaining what he

has lost, Fairchild decides to castrate himself, only to discover that he has made himself incapable of "wielding his revolver." Meanwhile, Galy Gay acquires the Widow Begbick as his reward and becomes an expert at handling — what else? — the machine gun.

This argument against individualism, and his explanation of a comic strategy based on collectivism, apparently found little response in the aftermath of the Hitler years, for in 1954, addressing himself once more to the problem of *Mann ist Mann*, Brecht felt obliged to qualify his earlier view by disapproving of the kind of society of which Galy Gay becomes part and of the way in which his newfound strength was exercised. Any performance of the play, he cautioned, should emphasize the negative aspects of his protagonist's "growth into criminality" and make clear that Galy Gay had been taken in by the wrong group. "Das Problem des Stückes," as he now saw it, "ist das falsche, schlechte Kollektiv (der 'Bande') und seine Verführungskraft . . ." [51] Obviously, the problem has shifted in his own mind from an individual to a social matter.

Among various "warning" interpretations of the play, the most interesting is contained in an imaginary dialogue (undated) between Brecht and a disgruntled playgoer. The fictional playgoer has just "wasted an evening" in the theater trying to make sense of Brecht's play and decides to take out his spleen on the author. Not only does *Mann ist Mann* fail to satisfy one's normal expectations from a play, he avers, it also violates one's cherished beliefs and assumptions about life, about man and God, about what is amusing or serious, about the power of ideals or the noble effects of a literary masterpiece, and so on and so forth. To

51. "The problem of the play is false or bad collectivity (represented by the 'gang') and its power of leading one astray." Brecht, *Gesammelte Werke*, 17:951.

each of these objections Brecht offers the same reply, first repeating his antagonist's exact words (an exasperating technique), then posing the ominous rhetorical question: "Was hilft dir [dies alles . . .] und es trifft dich ein glühendes Stück Eisen und löscht dich aus von der Welt und dem Leben?"[52] Indirectly, then, Brecht warns the playgoer that no values will be of much use if they cannot ward off eventual threats to one's very existence. At the end of the dialogue, Brecht has reduced his detractor to near hysteria. The poor fellow is prepared to admit that the play must really be good after all and its "message well worth reflecting on."

Now the warning given in this dialogue is rather more hortatory than cautionary; it suggests that forewarning is forearming and that foresight involves projection as well as prevention. What is at stake is a habit of mind — the kind of attitude or thought which prevents a man from recognizing reality in anything except that to which he has already grown accustomed. As mentioned earlier, Brecht was aware that a new way of thinking was prerequisite to a new way of doing and that fundamental change depended on a different conception about the nature of things. Along with everyone else in the twenties, especially the expressionists, he believed the world was in need of and ripe for a "new type of human being" and that it was his duty to assist in its formation. Hence his reason for portraying Galy Gay in a way that "would initially appear so strange and distasteful to contemporary playgoers." He wanted his audiences to be free of the usual theatrical illusion, that they were observing themselves or "an old acquaintance" in the protagonist, and imagine instead that they were witnessing "eine neue Art

52. "What good is all this to you if you're struck by a piece of red-hot iron and it obliterates you from the world and from life." Ibid., 7:979. This dialogue is found in pp. 978–80.

von Typus, vielleicht eben einen Vorfahren dieses neuen Typus Mensch, von dem ich gesprochen habe." [53] Galy Gay, then, was to show something of the qualities needed by the future man of Brechtian persuasion — not man as he might continue to evolve, but as he might develop or transform himself pragmatically in the light of present historical knowledge. As we have seen, Brecht was uncertain at the time about the form this new type might assume. He knew only that "Dieser neue Typus Mensch wird nicht so sein, wie ihn der alte Typus Mensch sich gedacht hat," and that "Er wird sich nicht durch die Maschinen verändern lassen, sondern er wird die Maschinen verändern, und wie immer er aussehen wird, vor allem wird er wie ein Mensch aussehen." [54] In short, the new man must be willing like Galy Gay to cast off what he was and modify his life according to contemporary need, but unlike Galy Gay he must act rather than be acted upon, must be aware of what he wants to become and of the means necessary to realize that aim. The fundamental problem was method: how to seize the initiative with respect to change so that instead of merely experiencing its effects, man would himself be able to plan and control the course of events according to an end in view.

This purpose is actually realized in *Mann ist Mann*, of course, but with results and procedures that Brecht professes to disapprove of! How are we to explain this? Why does he choose the soldiers as his instrument of change and what inferences are we to draw from the way they go

53. "A new kind of type, perhaps even a forerunner of the new type human being I mentioned." Brecht, "Vorrede zu *Mann ist Mann*," *Gesammelte Werke*, 7:977. The foreword was written for radio presentation over Sender Radio Berlin in March, 1927. Brecht was the speaker.
54. "This new type human being will not be the same as the old type of human being conceived of him. He will not let himself be changed by machines, but will change the machines himself. And however he looks, above all he will look like a human being." Ibid.

about it? Surely the most succinct answer is that only the
soldiers know what has to be done in the immediate circumstances and how to accomplish it. This accounts, at
first, for their immense advantage over Galy Gay. Where
he is unaware, they are utterly sure; where he hesitates,
they act; where he is passive, they are aggressive; and
where he is guileless, they have already sensed the lay of
the land. When they discover he has a weakness for ele-
phants, therefore, and fancies himself the right man for
any good deal, they simply concoct an appropriate piece
of business to trap him, "wie es in unserer Zeit üblich
ist." [55] Not only do the soldiers know their man, however,
they have also sized up the contemporary situation correctly and put themselves functionally in line with it.
Hence their occupation. Like the soldiers in *Mutter Cou-
rage*, which of course is a much later play, the machine
gun crew in *Mann ist Mann* accepts war as the natural
human condition and thinks of peace as a "time of disorder" intruding upon it. They don't question this fact, they
just take it for granted and act accordingly. Theirs not to
reason why, or to pass judgment on a matter, but simply
to appraise the immediate state of affairs and determine
the measures it calls for. Thus, they have no idea where
they might be fighting next — "Wenn sie Baumwolle brauchen, dann ist es Tibet, und wenn sie Schafwolle
brauchen, dann ist es Pamir" [56]; nor do they have a clear
image of their enemy, "denn es ist bis jetzt noch nicht
mitgeteilt worden." [57] Only two things are indispensable
to a soldier: his identification card, because it eliminates
doubt as to who he is or to what he belongs; and his man-
ual of arms, because it provides unshakeable authority as
to how he is to behave — "das einzige, an das man sich als

55. "As it is customary in our times."
56. "If cotton is needed it'll be Tibet; if wool is needed it'll be Pamir."
57. "Since it hasn't been announced yet."

Mensch halten kann, weil es Rückgrat gibt und die Ver-
antwortung vor Gott übernimmt."[58] Soldiers, then, are rationalized men in a completely rationalized profession,
with no other duty than to carry out their functions with
maximum efficiency. As such, they are the perfect instruments of anarchy and most in tune with the times: their
exclusive business is waging war by all organizable means.

The soldiers' advantage rests on a deteriorating historical situation. In an earlier phase of anarchy, as represented in *Von morgens bis mitternachts*, for example, rationalization had been confined to the separate spheres of
social existence without penetrating into the inner part of
man; human values lingered on as a hope or a memory
and it was still possible to believe in a reality beyond the
immediate state of affairs. Not so in *Mann ist Mann*. Here
only experience is real, there are no goals beyond an end
in view, there is no measure of things except the thing itself. The soldiers are "sachlich denkende Menschen in
einer sachlich denkenden Zeit."[59] When they reason, it is
by proceeding from A to B; when they act it is by the
numbers. Their language is neutralized to eliminate emotional and connotative intent; their imagery is drawn from
the world of technology and machines; and their truths
are tautological—formulas abstract enough to be valid
under a variety of conditions: "Mann ist Mann; Tempel ist
Tempel; Elefant ist Elefant; Geschäft ist Geschäft."[60] Anarchy has reached the ironical point of no return, its genius employed in the service of destruction, and reason is
used for purposes that contradict its own nature. The
outer limits of rationalization *and* of irrationality had both

58. "The only thing a man can depend on because it gives him back-
bone and takes over his responsibility before God."
59. "Men who think matter-of-factly in a matter-of-fact time."
60. "Man equals man; temple is temple; elephant is elephant; business
is business."

been reached: rationalization, because all means were directed towards an end prescribed by the immediate concatenation of circumstances; the irrational, because these circumstances are themselves the measure of value, because purpose is determined solely by the situation and morality solely by the efficient performance of function. What had once promised to be man's most effective instrument of change, his reason, now seemed to be applied against the qualities most characteristic of him as a human being.

Now in sizing up the historical state of affairs so accurately, I implied, Brecht took the first step towards "remoralizing" a situation already demoralized by inaccuracy. That is to say, he recognized that any strategy for coping with the situation would have to be based on the actual conditions and not, as was the case among his immediate predecessors, on something extraneous to those conditions. Again he was anti-expressionist, for expressionism had described the anarchic state only to deny it. Not able to find a way of dealing with the problem on its own terms, the expressionists looked for a solution outside the world of human affairs, positing an absolute realm of values divorced from the facts of nature and experience. Their strategies were transcendental or dialectical, designed to place a man beyond his situation and invent a role that would set him uniquely apart from the circumstances involved. For Brecht, on the other hand, experience is the only realm of possibilities, and historical developments alone provide a clue as to the operation of change. The contemporary situation was the result of rationalized procedures; therefore let reason also be applied to the solution of human problems. Since science had discovered how certain things are related to other things and had learned to manipulate nature accordingly, then the obvious step was to utilize its findings and apply its methods for one's own benefit. The proper strategy was to fight fire with fire: in more specific terms, to evaluate the soldiers' procedure and infer from it the why's and wherefore's of one's own actions according to the end in view.

Now the key to the soldiers' success lies in method — in the almost scientific logic and thoroughness of their operation. The foundation is a readiness to act on the knowledge provided by history. Jesse Mahoney, you recall, describes their experiment with Galy Gay as an "historic event," meaning not only that a unique happening is about to take place, but also that the moment in mankind's development has arrived where such an event becomes feasible. The old conceptions of character and personality are dead; new ones, incipiently at least, can be tested for their validity. Now is the time to deduce, and act upon, the ultimate consequences of the Copernican revolution, time to discard the so-called psychological probabilities and proceed functionally to explore the possibilities science has placed at man's disposal. When they set about their transformation of Galy Gay, therefore, it is to prove the validity of a thesis formulated only after repeated observations in the world of common sense, and they conduct it like an experiment in the laboratory with careful control of conditions and the greatest possible elimination of irrelevant factors. The soldiers have even "analyzed" the phenomenon with which they are dealing into its component elements, as the convergence of variables represented in the elephant image, thereby making it possible for them to substitute one variable for another, manipulating the structure of that phenomenon according to the formula with which they operate. In short, these technicians of anarchy have been able to transform human material because they accept the view that nature consists of events rather than substances and know that control over such events lies in determining their sequence, in making a *history* out of them by ensuring "a continuity of change from beginnings to endings." [61]

I have exaggerated the scientific parallel a bit — not further, I hope, than the evidence allows, but with somewhat more assurance perhaps than the author himself displays — in order to emphasize the pragmatic (historical, naturalistic) basis of Brecht's future strategic stance and to stress the illustrative nature of his "demonstration," including the possibility of learning from it and applying the point to one's own case. Nothing was more despicable to Brecht than an individual's waiting helplessly for unpredictable eventualities to overtake him; nothing more admirable than an individual's accepting the challenge to determine a course of events for himself by taking issue with a fictional example.

Mann ist Mann does offer such a challenge, made explicit by the Widow Begbick in quoting Brecht as to the theme or thesis of the play, but actually implicit in the title itself. "Ein Mann ist wie der andere: Mann ist Mann," [62] the soldiers claim, and for them, of course, this tautology is self-evident, true by virtue of the logical form in which it is cast. Yet must it really be taken at face value, or necessarily interpreted in the soldiers' way? After all, the two factors of the equation are not bound to be equal or identical; *Mann*, on the one side, might represent an individual and, on the other, the species — the one being merely a special instance of the other. In this case only certain qualities of man qua man would be interchangeable, not one person for another or the individual for his kind. Again, one man differs from another man although both remain Man, and each individual differs within himself at different times. He contains multipoten-

61. John Dewey, *Experience and Nature*, p. 139.
62. "One man is like the other; man equals man."

tialities, one or the other of which will emerge as dominant according to circumstances or according to the arrangement of those possibilities in a certain complex. Furthermore, from the standpoint of others, a man's identity lies in how he relates to them or what function he performs with respect to them. He becomes, like Galy Gay, what they conceive him to be, without surrendering his original essential qualities. To risk a mathematical analogy: the formula "man equals man" might be compared to the equation "four equals four," where it is quite obvious that the relationship so described might also be expressed as "two times two equals four" or "three plus one equals four" or "five minus one equals four," and so on ad libitum. Each individual expression is only a different functional variable of the same truth. The tautology holds, but only when allowance is made for infinite variations within it, depending on how the factors of the equation are defined and then related to each other. In sum, the formula is not prescriptive; it is simply a way of describing abstract possibilities. The soldiers demonstrate the method by which transformations can be made. It is up to us to determine what we might want to change and the direction of the process according to the end we might have in view.

Bibliography and Index

Bibliography

Babbitt, Irving. *Rousseau and Romanticism*. 1947. Reprint. Cleveland: World Publishing Co., Meridian, 1955.

Bentley, Eric. "On Brecht's *In the Swamp, A Man's a Man*, and *Saint Joan of the Stockyards*." In *Brecht: A Collection of Critical Essays*, edited by Peter Demetz. Englewood Cliffs, New Jersey: Prentice-Hall, A Spectrum Book, 1962.

————. *The Life of the Drama*. London: Methuen and Co., 1965.

Bergstraesser, Arnold. *Goethe's Image of Man and Society*. Chicago: Henry Regnery Co., 1949.

Böll, Heinrich. "Der Zeitgenosse und die Wirklichkeit." Lecture, Northwest German Radio. Cologne, 1953.

Brecht, Bertolt. *Gesammelte Werke*. 20 vols. Werkausgabe Edition. Edited by Elisabeth Hauptmann. Frankfurt am Main: Suhrkamp, 1967. "Bei Durchsicht meiner ersten Stücke" (March 1954) and "Vorrede zu *Mann ist Mann*" (April 1927) are in vol. 17.

————. *Stücke*. 12 vols. Edited by Elisabeth Hauptmann. vols. 1–2, *Erste Stücke*. Berlin: Suhrkamp, 1953. *Baal, Trommeln in der Nacht*, and *Im Dickicht der Städte* are found in vol. 1, *Mann ist Mann* in vol. 2.

Bridgwater, Patrick. "Hans Magnus Enzensberger." In *Essays on Contemporary German Literature*, edited by Brian Keith-Smith. German Men of Letters, vol. 4. London: Oswald Wolff, 1966.

Broch, Herman. *Gesammelte Werke*. 10 vols. Zurich: Rhein-Verlag, 1952–61. Vol. 2, *Die Schlafwandler*, edited by F. Stoessinger and A. Arendt.

Burke, Kenneth. *Attitudes towards History*. 2nd rev. ed. Boston: Beacon Press, 1959.

———. *A Grammar of Motives*. Englewood Cliffs, New Jersey: Prentice-Hall, 1945. Reprint. New York: George Brazillier, 1955.

———. *Permanence and Change: An Anatomy of Purpose*. With an Introduction by Hugh Dalziel Duncan. 2nd rev. ed. Indianapolis: Bobbs-Merrill, 1965.

———. *Perspectives by Incongruity*. Edited by Stanley Edgar Hyman. Bloomington: Indiana University Press, A Midland Book, 1964.

———. *The Philosophy of Literary Form: Studies in Symbolic Action*. Rev. ed., abridged by the author. New York: Random House, Vintage Books, 1957.

———. *Terms for Order*. Edited by Stanley Edgar Hyman. Bloomington: Indiana University Press, 1964.

Dewey, John. *Experience and Nature*. 2nd ed. New York: Dover Publications, 1958.

Diebold, Bernhard. "Georg Kaiser der Denkspieler." In *Anarchie im Drama*. Frankfurt am Main: Verlags-Anstalt, 1921.

Esslin, Martin. *Brecht: The Man and His Work*. Garden City, New York: Doubleday and Co., 1960.

———. *The Theater of the Absurd*. Garden City, New York: Doubleday and Co., Anchor Books, 1961.

Fontane, Theodor. *Causerien über Theater*. 3rd ed. Edited by Paul Schlenther. Berlin: F. Fontane and Co., 1905.

Goethe, Johann Wolfgang von. "Dämon" in "Urworte. Orphisch." *Werke*. Sophien Edition. 133 vols. Weimar: Hermann Böhlaus, 1887–1919. Ser. 1, vol. 41, 1902.

Gray, Ronald. *Bertolt Brecht*. New York: Grove Press, Evergreen Edition, 1961.

Hauptmann, Gerhart. *Gesammelte Werke.* 8 vols. Jubiläumsausgabe. S. Fischer Verlag: Berlin, 1921. *Einsame Menschen* is in vol. 1.

Holz, Arno. "Kunsttheoretische Schriften." *Werke.* Neuwied, Berlin: Hermann Luchterhand Verlag, 1961–64. In vol. 5. Edited by Wilhelm Emrich and Anita Holz.

Hyman, Stanley Edgar. *The Armed Vision: A Study in the Methods of Literary Criticism.* Rev. ed., abridged by the author. New York: Random House, Vintage Books, 1955.

Kaiser, Georg. *Von morgens bis mitternachts.* Stück in zwei Teilen. Fassung letzter Hand. Edited and with a Postscript by Walther Huder. Stuttgart: Reclam, Universal-Bibliothek, 1965.

Keith-Smith, Brian, ed. *Essays on Contemporary German Literature.* German Men of Letters, vol. 4. London: Oswald Wolff, 1966.

Kutscher, Artur. *Frank Wedekind: Sein Leben und seine Werke.* 3 vols. Munich: Georg Müller, 1922. Vol. 1.

Niebuhr, Reinhold. *Beyond Tragedy: Essays on the Christian Interpretation of History.* New York: Charles Scribner's Sons, 1937.

O'Connor, William Van. *Sense and Sensibility in Modern Poetry.* Chicago: University of Chicago Press, 1948.

Schopenhauer, Arthur. "Über die Grundlage der Moral." In *Sämtliche Werke.* Großherzog Wilhelm Ernst Edition. 5 vols. Leipzig: Insel Verlag, n.d. Vol. 3.

Schwab-Felisch, Hans, ed. *Gerhart Hauptmann: Die Weber.* Dichtung und Wirklichkeit. Frankfurt am Main: Ullstein, 1963.

Sokel, Walter H. *The Writer in Extremis: Expressionism in Twentieth-Century German Literature.* Stanford: Stanford University Press, 1959.

Szondi, Peter. *Theorie des modernen Dramas.* Frankfurt am Main: Suhrkamp, 1966.

Wedekind, Frank. *Prosa, Dramen, Verse.* 2nd ed. Munich: Langen-Müller, 1960.

Weisinger, Herbert. *Tragedy and the Paradox of the Fortunate Fall.* London: Routledge and Kegan Paul, 1953.

Index

Absurd: in Brecht, 131, 134–35, 141; Theatre of the, 132

Actuality: relation of to reality, 4, 13, 18–19, 39; tradition of, in German drama, 12–13, 17; use of, in the documentary play, 12, 13–14; criticism of use in drama, 39

—in Brecht: 120–21

—in Hauptmann: 24–25, 27–29

—in Kaiser: rejection of, 70–71; attempt to realize ideal in, 104

—in Wedekind: nondeterminative of reality, 49, 56; interpretation of, 56–57

Aktualität, 4, 13. *See also* Actuality

Alienation: characteristic of anarchy, 79; crime as protest against, 87–88; of artist, in anarchy, 89, 103; Kaiser's solution for, 112–13

Alienation effect. *See Verfremdungseffekt*

Anarchy, age of: responses to by Kaiser and Brecht, 18, 66; central problem in, 91; concept of

poet in, 122–24; compared with Brecht, 125–26

—in Brecht: as background to work, 122, 126; soldiers as representative of, 163–64, 166–67; extreme limits in, 164–65

—in Kaiser: as background to work, 76–79; complementary aspects of, 85; counterideal to, 91; scenically represented, 111–12; portrait of poet in, 122–23

Anderswerden: in era of transition, 36–37, 147; as part of situation in Hauptmann, 36, 142

Aristotle, 47

Authority: crisis of, at turn of century, 21–22; in Hauptmann, 25, 34, 78; in Wedekind, 58, 78; in Kaiser, 78–79; in Brecht, 122

Baal (Brecht), 118–19, 124–26

Baudelaire, Charles (1821–1867), 125

Bismarck, Otto, Fürst von (1815–1898), 21, 64

Böll, Heinrich (1917–): concepts

Index 181

festation at puberty, 53–54, as life-force, 59, as norm for morality, 57, 61, 144; in Brecht, 125

Negation: in Kaiser, as aspect of strategy, 84, 99, 100–101, 109, reflected in crime, 88, manifested in semantic pun, 95; in Brecht, 125, 157

Neue Mensch, der: Kaiser's conception of, 73, 106, 121; Brecht's version of, 161–62. *See also* Martyr; Rebirth pattern

Nietzsche, Friedrich (1844–1900), 21, 44

Nossack, Hans Erich (1901–), 11

Paradox: in Kaiser, as aspect of strategy, 93, 95, 99, 105, as characteristic of situation, 96–99, in rebirth pattern, 102, in martyrdom, 107–8. *See also Felix culpa*, myth of; Semantic pun

Parody, 46

Personality: concept of, at issue in Brecht, 149; Goethe's view of, 150–52; twentieth-century idea of, 153–54

Perspective-by-incongruity: compared to *Verfremdungseffekt*, 135; definition of, 135–36

Politics: and documentary play, 16–18

Power: in Kaiser, related to creativity, 91, 109, fraudulent use of, 104, symbolized by money, 108–9; in Brecht, 158–60

Proverbs: as names for recurrent situations, 8; Brecht's use of, 120

Psychology: of the poetic act, 9; and behaviorism, 153–54

Puberty: symbol in Wedekind for transition, 52–54; as natural reality, 56–57

Purgatory: in Kaiser, experience as, 104–5, 106

Rationalization
—in anarchy: joined with irrationality, 164–65
—in Brecht: aspect of anarchy, 122; and irrationality, 165
—in Kaiser: as characteristic of anarchy, 79; false strategy in reaction to, 82, 88
—in Wedekind: equated with formula for living, 51–52, 60–63, 144; compared with Freud's technique, 62–63; idea of, exemplified in artiste, 64–65

Realdichtung, 64

Realität, 4, 13, 51. *See also* Reality

Reality: relationship to actuality, 4, 7, 13, 39; as orientation or interpretation, 7, 13; turn of century crisis in nature of, 20–22; Kaiser's view of, 70–71; in age of anarchy, 76–79; based on substantival view of nature, 151–53; altered by functional view of nature, 153–54
—in Hauptmann: centered in historical conditions, 33–34; leading to mode of compromise, 45
—in Wedekind: not located in actuality, 49; symbolized by puberty, 51; as universal experience, 56–57; as real forces of existence, 59; morality as concomitant of, 60–61

Rebirth pattern: in Kaiser, 81, 83–85, 102–3; and concept of martyr, 108

Reinhardt, Max (1873–1943), 49

Rimbaud, Arthur (1854–1891), 125

Romanticism: in Brecht, 125, 127; in Kaiser, 145–46; and science, 145

Sachlichkeit, Neue, 164–65

Sacrifice: in tragic process, 75; in Kaiser's strategy, 84, 86, 106;